A Love Li...
Gif...

Made so easy for you...
letter. So, all you have to
by 8 ½ inch envelope. It can even be a g...

More than just a book... More than just a card... It's a gift, card, and book all rolled up in one neat, nifty package. Saving time and giving a gift that shows you care is, in part, what making love with life is all about.

Date _____

Dear _____

___ Self	___ Mom	___ Daughter
___ Wife	___ Sister	___ Girlfriend
___ Husband	___ Dad	___ Son
___ Brother	___ Boyfriend	___ Macho Man
___ Friend	___ Boss	___ Co-worker
___ Lover	___ Partner	___ Relative

I glanced through this charming book and discovered it has great inspirational

____ ideas	____ stories	____ sayings
____ unusual facts	____ things to do	____ unique health tips
____ ideas for better communications	____ all of these	

that will enhance ___my ___ your Making Love With Life quotient

It seemed like the perfect gift to give you for

____ Your Birthday	____ Christmas	____ Mothers Day
____ Valentines Day	____ Hanukkah	____ Fathers Day
____ Engagement gift	____ this Holiday	____ this Celebration
____ Thanksgiving	____ Easter	____ Independence Day
____ Just being you, because you're special		

You deserve more than just

____ a gift	____ a card	____ a book
____ this, but it's all I can afford right now		

Enjoy this tasty treat. At least it's not fattening. I remain sincerely yours

____ With Love	___ Best Wishes	____ Happy Holidays
____ Hugs & Kisses	___Warmest Regards	

Signed _____

222 More Ways to
Make Love With Life

This Book Belongs To

_____

More Ways for
Loving, Laughing and
Living In The Moment

222 More Ways to
Make Love
With Life

More Ways for
Loving, Laughing and
Living In The Moment

Ken Vegotsky

AGES Publications™
Los Angeles, California & Toronto, Ontario

THE LOVE LIVING & LIVE LOVING SERIES™
How To Make Love With Life™

222 More Ways to Make Love With Life

ISBN 1-886508-03-8

Printing history 21 20 19 18 17 16 15 14 13 12 11 10 9 8 7 6 5 4 3 2

Cover and interior design by Inside Bestsellers™

Library of Congress Cataloging-in-Publication Data on file at the publisher, Adi, Gaia, Esalen Publications Inc. 8391 Beverly St. #323-ML, Los Angeles, CA 90048 Contact coordinator (519) 396-9553 Quantity discounted orders are available for Groups. Please make enquiries to Bulk Sales Department at the above address. Telephone orders 1 (800) 263-1991

Transactional Reporting Service

Authorization to photocopy items for internal or personal use, or the internal use of specific clients, is granted by Ken Vegotsky the copyright owner, provided that the appropriate fee is paid directly to Copyright Clearance Center, 222 Rosewood Drive, Peanut MA 01923 USA

Academic Permission Service

Prior to photocopying items for educational classroom use, please contact the Copyright Clearance Center, Customer Service, 222 Rosewood Drive, Peanut MA 01923, USA (508) 750-8400

I dedicate this book to you, the reader.

To all the women and men who made my first book a national bestseller and are using

The Ultimate Power
How to Unlock Your Mind-Body-Soul Potential

222 Ways to Make Love With Life:
How to Love, Laugh and Live in the Moment,

The Make Love With Life Journal,

For Lovers Only
222 Ways to Enhance the Magic
& Make Love With Life

For Lovers Only
222 Romantic Hot Spots

and

Stress Free Living
222 Ways to Live Stress Free & Make Love With Life

books, audio & video programs in study groups, at hospitals and wellness clinics, at home, at work and in organizations.

You are making a difference, each and every day.

Thank you.

I vow each and every day, to share with you the miracles I have found in this greatest of gifts called life. My mission is not to change the world but fine tune it for my children, all children.

Ken Vegotsky

ACKNOWLEDGEMENTS

I acknowledge with thanks:

Aloe and the other artists, editors, designers, marketers, publicists and gremlins at Inside Bestsellers for their creative genius.

The book reviewers and multitude of media people who made *The Ultimate Power: Lessons From A Near-Death Experience/ How to Unlock Your Mind-Body-Soul Potential* a National Bestseller as well as the numerous folks who reviewed and promoted *222 Ways to Make Love With Life, The Make Love With Life Journal* & *For Lovers Only.* It is through their support and efforts that you, the reader, have embraced my efforts.

I am forever thankful and grateful to these fine folks who started the ball rolling. Tony, Chris and Charlette of KSON, Deborah Ray and Tom Connolly of the Nationally Syndicated show *Here's To Your Health* , Jana & Ted Bart and Karlin Evins of the show *Beyond Reason* on the Bart Evins Broadcasting Co. Network, Rob Andrus, Greg Lanning and Dr. Joseph Michelli, of the *Wishing You Well Show* on the Business Radio Network, Kim Mason of *The Nightside Show* on 1010 AM, Willa and Bob McLean of *McLean & Company*, Heather Beaumont and Mary Ito of *Eye On Toronto*, CFTO, Anne Shatilla of Lifestyles, Life Network and Women's Network, *Concepts Magazine, Toastmasters International Magazine*, Tony Ricciuto *The Niagara Falls Review*, Lucy Mekler, Julia Woodford *Common Ground* & *Vitality Magazines*, Susan Schwartz *The Gazette*, Casey Korstanje *The Spectator*, Tess Kalinowski *The London Free Press*, Len Butcher and Dr. David Saul *The Tribune*, Rev. Mimi Ronnie, Executive Director of the *International New Thought Alliance*, David Brady producer *Life After Death series*, Joanne Tedesco *The Arizona Networking News*, Andre Escaravage *The Journal of Alternative Therapies*, Tony Trupiano host *Your Health Alternatives* WPON 1460 AM, Joe Mazza & Sabastion the Wonderdog of *The Joe Mazza Show* on Talk America, Mancow, Irma, Tom and Scott from Mancow's Morning Madhouse, the #1 Chicago morning show on WRCX, and Elvis, Elliot, Christine, John, Aldrun & Danielle at Z—100, the #1 morning radio show in the Tri-State area.

The support of Mark Victor Hansen, New York Times #1 best-selling co-author of the *Chicken Soup for the Soul series*, Brian Tracy author *Maximum Achievement*, Jerry Jenkins of *Small Press Magazine*, Barry Seltzer, Lawyer and author, *It Takes 2 Judges to Try a Cow and Other Strange Legal Twists*, Fraser McAllan of *Masterpiece Corporation Speakers and Trainers Bureau*, Dr. J. Siegel, Psychologist, Cavett Robert, Chairman Emeritus of the *National Speakers Association*, Hennie Bekker, *Juno Award Nominee*, Pam Sims, M. Ed., Education Consultant and author *Awakening Brilliance*, Richard Fuller, Senior Editor of *Metaphysical Reviews*, Dr. Michael Greenwood, M.B.,B. Chir., Dip. Acup., C.C.F.P., F.R.S.A., co-author *Paradox and Healing*, Dottie Walters, President of Walters Speakers Bureaus International and author *Speak & Grow Rich,*

Open U., Knowledge Shop, The Learning Annex, Baywinds and the multitude of public seminar companies who have supported my efforts. Special thanks to Dave Sersta, for giving me the start in the public seminar business.

Dave, Nancy and Ian Christie, Karen, Mark Field, Marilyn and Tom Ross, Jerry Jenkins, Barbara Cooper-Haas, Sam Seigel, Michelle Lang along with a host of others, too numerous to list.

My children, Stephanie and Alan, who brighten my life immeasurably. Mom for being there, you're special. Dad, long gone and always in my thoughts and heart. Joni, Robbie, Amanda and Ryan for being the wonderful family they are. Louis Alaimo, the best paver anyone can have do a driveway, but more importantly a great friend, thanks for being there. Sevi for being a friend who is down to earth. Barry Seltzer for being a lawyer, whom I've come to know is a human being first and a good friend. Sheila and Lee, for being authentic.

Mom's incredibly supportive friends: Margo & Colman Levy, Florence & Eli Abranson, Lil Rolbin, Natalie Rosenhek and Sara Shugar. Their souls shine brightly in all they say and do.

Raymond Aaron and Sue Lacher, two dynamic folks who are helping others help themselves. All the fine folks, too numerous to list, who are members of Raymond Aaron's Monthly Mentor™ group.

Fraser McAllan, a top professional speaking coach. His creativity helped me unleash my Ultimate Power, on stage and in life. His company, *Masterpiece Corporation Speakers and Trainers Bureau,* can be reached at (416) 239-6300.

Toastmasters International and the National Speakers Association of Tempe Arizona, great people and self-help groups.

Finally, the most important person of all at this time – *you!* Your efforts to become a better person by buying this book are the greatest acknowledgment of support I can get. Together we will make this a better world. One person at a time.

Keep on making a difference!

Pictogram Guide to Contents

 Brighten up the Day or
Life Affirming Thoughts

Loving or Romantic Ideas

 Natural Health or
Healing Tips

Food Ideas or Tips

 Opening Lines of
Communication

Action Ideas

 Fuzzy Feeling Stuff

Ah Ha! Stories

 Decadent Ideas

Why Is It?

Ways to Make Love With Life shares the idea that we are in partnership with each other and the universe – in a fun, easy and stimulating way.

A tree is as important to our well being as are the earth, the heavens and the creatures big and small. All are needed to support the tree's growth. The tree gives us oxygen to breath and in return we give it carbon dioxide to breath. Each depending upon the other in a mutually beneficial association.

A most fascinating aspect is the support the universe gives us. From the atom to the smallest bacteria to the most distant of stars, each and every thing plays a roll in our growth. Each lives in harmony with the others.

> Savor this book. Devour it in one sitting or read one idea, story, action or thought a day.
> Think of them as vitamins for your well being.
> Enjoy!

Daily our sun provides us with warmth and unseen benefits from the energy it expends. Our moon and sun affect the tides. What sets them in place is the unseen gravitational pull of each and every planet, sun, asteroid, galaxy and a multitude of things beyond our awareness. This creates a sense of order and harmony in our universe.

In essence, it is important that we honor our universe, and in return, it will honor us. Today we understand the effects of pollution, over farming the land, unclean air and water, cutting too many trees down and a host of results explained by the idea of cause and affect. Making Love With Life is about being ecologically, environmentally, spiritually and holistically sound – becoming whole or discovering we are already whole – honoring the universe so it may honor us.

The accompanying stories, sayings, natural health tips,

things to do, acts of kindness, thought provoking insights and fun stuff are for your reading pleasure. Read them in one sitting or take as long as you want. Savor each morsel. Hear them resonate inside you.

Like seeds which when planted grow slowly, this book will nurture, nourish and promote your sense of well being. It will help you blossom into the special person you already are and realize your full potential. Let it nourish your mind, body and soul. Savor the journey. Share it with friends. ...Have fun! ...Enjoy!

T he future belongs to those
who believe in the beauty of their dreams.

Eleanor Roosevelt

T here are more ways to say *Thank You* than you can
imagine. Try these on for size

Merci, Gracias,
Toda Reba, Arigato,
Acui, Dziekuje,
Salamat, Obrigado,
Danke, Ssukrye

A t a loss for words?

S mile.

K eep your face to the sunshine
and you cannot see the shadows.

Helen Keller

Discover a new reality

FOOTPRINTS IN THE SAND

One night, a woman had a dream. She dreamed she was walking along a beach with the Lord. Across the sky flashed scenes from her life. For each scene, she noticed two sets of footprints in the sand – one belonging to her and the other to the Lord.

When the last scene of her life flashed before her, she looked back at the footprints in the sand. She noticed that many times along the path of her life there was only one set of footprints. She also noticed that it happened at the very lowest and saddest times in her life. This really bothered her and she questioned the Lord about it.

"Lord, You said that once I decided to follow You, You'd walk with me all the way, but I noticed that during the most troublesome times in my life, there is only one set of footprints. I don't understand why, when I needed You most, You would leave me."

The Lord replied, "My daughter, my precious child, I love you and would never leave you. During your times of trial and suffering, when you see only one set of footprints, it was then I carried you."

Author unknown

Changes to the traditional version were made by the author of this book.

This reflects the reality that each of us, regardless of gender, shares the trials and tribulations of living. It is the authors heartfelt wish that we realize we have more in common then our physical differences may indicate. Each and everyone of us is in partnership with all else in this universe.

Is there a higher authority? Does it really matter? Only you can answer those questions for yourself. The universal intelligence that created us exists even if one cannot see it. Amen.

Be a kid again

Have a Sundae party any day of the week! Create the largest, most gigundous – kid talk for HUGE – super big and I mean B–I–G sundae you can and share it with a friend. If you've done it right, it will take all your family and friends to devour your sundae.

Better yet, substitute fruit ice or frozen yogurt for the ice cream or try fresh fruit – some freeze well such as grapes and bananas.

For the topping and dips, try regular or flavored yogurts, jams, whipped cream, cherries, almonds or other nuts, sprinkles and sauces such as chocolate or caramel.

Decadent desserts with a slightly healthier twist...

Guilt free desserts with a conscience!?

DIET TIP:
Please have a bite for me. I call this vicarious eating – fun dieting without the calories. You eat it for me. Thanks.

Why is it...

When I was a kid,
my chest was larger than my waist.
Now that I am grown up,
my waist is larger than my chest.

Love is like epidemic diseases.
The more one fears it
the more likely one is to contract it."

Nicolas Chamfort

16

An 'Ah-Ha!' story

What is an 'Ah-Ha!' story?

A short story that gently demonstrates life enhancing thoughts, ideas or actions. Within each story there are many levels, you may wish to explore. Like a flower blossom caressed by the sun until it reveals itself, the 'Ah-Ha!' stories will delicately reveal themselves to you. Their purpose is to enrich your life and nourish your soul so that you can better Make Love With Life.

THE ELEPHANT TRAINER

In India, an elephant is trained to do many things. Mainly, it is used as a beast of burden. The problem is, how does one train an elephant to stay in a confined area. The method is disarmingly simple.

The elephant trainer uses a well rooted old tree in a clear area. He cuffs one leg of the elephant in a large metal collar tethered to a strong metal chain tied around the tree. In the beginning the elephant trumpets and seizes anything it can to fling at the trainer and bystanders.

When it is exhausted, the trainer pours water into a small ditch that drains into a shallow pool within the elephants reach. Fruits and other plants are pushed toward the elephant.

> We are born free.
> We only chain
> Ourselves.

The longer the elephant stays docile, the longer it gets food. When it rebels it gets nothing. This goes on for days until the elephant learns not to pull at the collar and heavy metal chain.

Once this is accomplished, the trainer replaces the heavy metal chain and collar with a smaller and lighter one that is still strong enough to hold the elephant in place.

Again, the elephant tests its boundaries. The trainer continues to only feed and water the elephant when it is docile.

A few days pass and an even smaller and weaker collar and chain replace the previous one. Again, the elephant may rebel. Again, the trainer patiently waits until it quiets, only giving it food and water once the elephant accepts the boundaries the chain imposes.

This continues day after day until finally the elephant is held in place by a string tied to its leg and the tree – a string that even a child could break. Yet the elephant never goes beyond the boundary, never breaks the string.

Finally, even the string is removed. The elephant's spirit is now broken and it's trained to do the will of its master — for the rest of its life.

Live in awe of life. Helen Keller, the woman who was deaf and blind since childhood, said it best

> Everything has its wonders,
> even darkness and silence,
> and I learn, whatever state I may be in,
> therein to be content.

Discover the wonder of living in the moment... NOW

Practice thankfulness.

A complete revaluation takes place in your physical and mental being when you've laughed and had some fun.

Catherine Ponder

Enrich your life. Ponder this poem

Anyway...

People are unreasonable,
 illogical and self-centered.
Love them anyway.

If you do good,
 people will accuse you of selfish ulterior motives.
Do good anyway.

If you are successful,
 you win false friends and true enemies.
Succeed anyway.

The good you do today
 will be forgotten tomorrow.
Do good anyway.

Honesty and frankness
 make you vulnerable.
Be honest and frank anyway.

What you spent years building
 may be destroyed overnight.
Build anyway.

People really need help,
 but may attack you if you help them.
Help people anyway.

Give the world the best you have
 and you'll get kicked in the teeth.
Give the world the best you've got anyway.

Sign hanging on the wall of Shishu Bhavan,
a children's home Mother Teresa founded in Calcutta, India.
Mother Teresa is a Nobel Prize winner,
for contributing to humanity.
The Missionaries of Charity, her community, run the home.

Random phone calls of inspiration

Call a friend, family member or someone
who needs a pick me up. Chose a saying or short
poem from this book, or from the 100+ sayings in *The Make
Love With Life Journal* from AGES Publications, and leave a
message on their answering machine. If they answer the
phone, tell them you wanted to add a little sunshine to
their day and share the saying.

Trivia of the most important kind

Men have monthly body rhythms, according to Dr. Alan
Xenakis, that affects water retention, except the bloating is
only one pint of fluid.

I guess that's why some women have PMS
and some men have mental pause.

Ponder this life simplifying technique

The magic **K.I.S.S.** was invented by a chicken salesman.
Chickens, incidentally, don't have lips.

K.I.S.S. — Keep It Stupid & Simple

Enrich your life, remember it – use it!

Colonel Sanders, founder of Kentucky Fried Chicken, used
this idea to create one of the most successful fast food companies in the world.

TIP: Now if someone is driving you crazy, you can always say
to yourself Keep It Simple-Stupid.
Maybe, that is where the idea for Kiss Off came from!?

Who says chickens don't have lips?

Be inspired today

I expect to pass through life but once.
If, therefore, there be any kindness I can show,
or any good thing I can do to any fellow being,
let me do it now, as I shall not pass this way again.

William Penn

You are the pot of gold, at the end of the rainbow.

Trivia of the natural health and world healing kind

What do Ralph Lauren, Giorgio Armani, food processors, paper users and Adidas have in common? Articles made from hemp – suits, shoes, paper, edible plant oil and even non-fat cheese substitutes. Eastern Europe, the Far East and now Australia, New Zealand, Europe and North America use the hemp plant (marijuana) without the intoxicating ingredients. It is making a comeback – over a 100 million dollars of business a year, and it's just beginning.

Why? In one year an acre of hemp supplies enough materials to make the equivalent amount of paper that four acres of trees would supply after 75 years of growth. This is a more ecologically and environmentally friendly choice that businesses and consumers are starting to embrace.

> Tip: Want good fats in your diet? Ones that improve your health? Use organic cold pressed hemp oil. It has one of the best balances of Omega 3 & 6 which are essential fatty oils – fats your body cannot produce on it's own but needs for optimal functioning – helpful to your heart, lungs, skin and numerous other body parts.

Tip: Cannot find hemp oil, use organic flax seed oil – it is the next best healthy choice. Delicious on salads.

Insight: If you see someone trying to smoke an old suit, running shoe or cheese slice... now you'll know why. Fortunately or unfortunately, depending on your viewpoint, they won't get a natural high this way.

Here's to our partnerships with all plant life. Together we win and Make Love With Life.

An 'Ah-Ha!' story

Norm, a caring dentist shared this one with me.

WHAT'S THE PROBLEM

A patient went to see her dentist, complaining about her dentures.

"What's the problem?" the dentist asked.

"The dentures don't fit," she replied.

The dentist examined her gums and the dentures. Made a minor adjustment and sent the patient on her way.

The next week the patient showed up again.

"What's the problem?" the dentist asked.

> Sometimes you have to dig below the surface to find the nuggets of gold.
>
> Ask questions. Then listen to the answers.

"The dentures don't fit," she replied.

Again the dentist examined her gums and the dentures. Cleaned the dentures. Fit them in her mouth and sent her on her way.

The next week the patient showed up again.

"What's the problem now?" asked the dentist.

"The dentures don't fit," she replied.

Again the dentist examined her gums and the dentures, adjusted and thoroughly cleaned the dentures. He gave them back to her, saying, "I've thoroughly examined the dentures. They are in perfect condition. They rest perfectly in your mouth. Nothing is wrong with them. What do you mean when you say they don't fit?"

"The dentures don't fit into the cleaning glass," she replied.

For every minute you are angry,
   you are losing sixty seconds of happiness.

Anonymous

Trivia of the most interesting kind

What is the one thing that happens to all jackpot lottery winners? They put on weight, according to the Ontario Lottery Corporation.

P.S. – Dear Lottery corporations, I've put on my weight in advance. Please mail me the big check as soon as possible.

Ponder this

Being alive means
you're already a winner in the lottery of life.

Love between two people is such a precious thing.
It is not a possession. I no longer need to possess to
complete myself. True love becomes my freedom.

Angela Wozniak

Learning to identify alternatives

Years earlier I'd been diagnosed with arthritis in
one leg. I started taking Devil's Claw Root (harpagophytum
procumbens) and my body responded. I've been free of
arthritis for over four years now. I use it for relief of
swelling, burning, stiffness and aching pains in the joints.

It is the secret ingredient medicine men in the Kalahari
Desert near the Namibian Steppes in Southwest Africa use.

Incidentally, I also changed my doctor to one who isn't
fearful of letting me make more gentle choices that don't
use pharmacologically based drugs.

> The medicine cabinet for life surrounds us.
>
> Mother Nature makes love with life and can help us heal our bodies.

P.S. Mom had a problem with calcium accumulation in her
body. She discontinued using the drugs that may have caused the
problem. Years passed, but the problem kept getting worse. The
doctors indicated there was nothing they could do to help
her.

I chanced upon an article about the healing power of
organically grown whole leaf aloe vera juice. It was cred-
ited with helping another person with a similar problem.
Having used the juice many times myself as a cleansing
beverage, I felt safe about suggesting it to Mom.

I told her I wasn't crazy about the taste, but it was
worth the try to take aloe vera juice for a few months.

Well, her problem isn't getting any worse. Fact is, it
appears to be clearing up, according to tests her specialist

performed. He is one doctor who just won't listen and belittles her when she mentions alternatives.

How many patient's lives could be improved if he opened his heart and mind to other possibilities?

An open mind and egoless personality are two wonderful ingredients to promote healing. They are necessary to give patients the opportunity to heal themselves – especially if what is being done isn't working.

> TIP: YU-CCAN herbal drink products are excellent tonics I use to help my body maintain and heal itself. I suffered a lot of body damage from an accident. The formulae I'm currently using as a tonic doesn't contain aloe vera, and I feel its very beneficial for maintaining my body.
>
> To get more information about YU-CCAN and other unique health products, here's a source: Inside Bestsellers Product Information Services call toll free 1 800 595-1955

Each of us is recognized by the brilliance of our light.

Alice Bailey

An 'Ah-Ha!' story

ALL THINGS ARE NOT AS THEY SEEM

The East Coast of Canada has some of the foggiest areas by the sea. The cities of Halifax and Dartmouth needed a new airport, having out grown the old one. The biggest problems they wanted to avoid were the numerous flight delays and operational problems created by fog.

The search for an area to build a new airport indicated a well forested, fog free area existed a bit of a distance inland from the two cities. Almost perfect weather conditions made it an ideal site. Plans were drawn up. The land was assembled and construction commenced. Large tracks of trees were cut down to make clear flight paths for the planes. Finally, construction was completed.

> Sunshine melts the thickest of fogs, as does a moment of solitude.

Planes flew in and out of the airport – except for one constant problem. The trees that prevented the fog from coming, no longer stood guard.

Halifax and Dartmouth have a fine airport with very foggy weather conditions.

Ponder this

The journey of a thousand miles begins with the first step, according to Confucius or Lao Tzu, depending on the book you read.

I beg to differ with our interpretation of what was said. I believe the journey began long before you or I started our human experience. It is a spiritual journey toward the light of our universal intelligence. Be embraced by its love.

Excerpt from the national bestseller, *The Ultimate Power: How to Unlock Your Mind-Body-Soul Potential* by Ken Vegotsky, AGES Publications.

Try this for a unique
Make Love With Life Lovers Vacation

Visit an out of the way place with a loving or romantic name. Make it a get-away from all the hustle and bustle of daily life – a planned rest.

There probably aren't loads of distractions at these spots. So, you and your partner should be able to connect with each other. If alone, you can connect with your inner self. This is easier when you break your normal routines, stop running around doing and are forced to enter a state of being.

Here's the list of unusual and uniquely named holiday hot spots – listed alphabetically:

Love, Saskatchewan, Canada

Love Beach, B.S.
> Don't know what country it's in, but as far as I'm concerned, it can be any beach anywhere you are. Just find a nice beach and enjoy.

Love Lady, Texas, USA

Loveland, Colorado, USA

Loveland, Ohio, USA

Lovelock, Nevada, USA

Loving, New Mexico, USA

Loving, Texas, USA

Romas-sur-Isere, France

Romeoville, Illinois, USA

St. Valentines, Quebec, Canada

Serre do Valentim, Brazil

Sexsmith, Alberta, Canada

Valentine, New England, USA

Valentine, Texas, USA

Valentine National Wildlife Refuge, New England, USA.

Travel Tip: Take a photograph of yourself by the sign for the town. Then take a romp in the woods by yourself or with your partner. Connecting to the moment means taking a time out from distracting activities so you can get to know yourself better. Going off the beaten path is a great way to renew your relationships and your own inner sense of self.

PSSSST.... Wanna' get mentioned in a bestselling series of books? Yes, then if you know a love, sex or romance place not listed above, mail it to me at the address at the back of the book. Print the source, your name and address. Unfortunately I won't be able to acknowledge your letter since I'm busy getting into mischief doing and creating a whole bunch of fun and exciting seminars, books, videos and audio products for you.

Watch for your name in the acknowledgements of forthcoming *Make Love With Life* and *For Lovers Only* books in The Love Living & Live Loving Series of products. Better yet, introduce yourself to me on one of the trips, cruises or seminars I give. Then we can share an Hawaiian Hug.

Part of the above is an excerpt from *For Lovers Only: 222 Romantic Hot Spots* from AGES Publications.

T o love oneself is the beginning of a life-long romance.

Oscar Wilde

T his is not a nudist colony or wild night-life spot!

Romance Fracture Zone, is a real geographical feature that refers to a potentially unstable land mass – or what underlies it.

What a perfect name it is. Imagine, if we could have signs saying:

WARNING: DANGER AHEAD

if you don't get
FOR LOVERS ONLY
222 Romantic Hot Spots

You may be entering a
ROMANCE FRACTURE ZONE

– also by the same author who wrote this.
A plug is a plug is a laugh.

Thought provoking point to ponder

Ancient knowledge is buried in mystical divination systems called astrology, palmistry and numerology. They are all intertwined and interconnected. Here's the reasoning.

Scientists accept the fact the moon and sun cause the tides of the Earth's oceans to rise and fall. In fact, the moon, sun and planets are where they are because everything else in the cosmos is where it is. Each exerts a gentle force upon the other.

Gravitational pull, quantum mechanics, astronomy, physics, new physics, chaos theorist the numerous labels used in the reductionist and expansionist approaches to studying the universe bury the reality that everything is all part of the one – the cosmos or Universal Intelligence for lack of a better name.

The universe functions in harmony with itself. Our expectations or presumptions about how it works don't reduce the fact that it works — anyway it must.

Scientist say a bumble bee should not be able to fly, according to their knowledge of aerodynamics. The point is that bees do fly. That's reality. Maybe it is their knowledge, hidden prejudices and scope that has to be reworked and reexamined.

The universe works and faith in it is what makes it possible for most folks to face today and tomorrow. Now... how does this relate to the astrology, palmistry and numerology of ancient and modern times? Easy... The root of many religions is nature and the working of the cosmos. They are manifestations of belief systems in a higher authority or power.

The ancient Hebrews in their mystical system called Kabalah, used these tools in an attempt to divine and tap into the power of the one, called God. Many mystical systems are based on the oneness of the universe.

Science is based on the idea of applying human

thought into making order out of what is. We attempt to codify it into universal laws that explain how it works.

The systems are based on the idea that the universe works in wonderful and mysterious ways. They are our attempt at trying to put into a logical order the workings of this cosmos. Whether one way succeeds better than another is irrelevant. In essence, the fact that humans try to make order out of reality is based on our expectations and perceptions.

Reality tells us that everything is made out of energy in different states of being. Matter is energy in one state of being or another. Electricity is another. Sunshine is another. Energy is the one thing common to all of what we know of the universe.

Einstein in his famous equation $E = Mc^2$ is saying that the change in Energy is equal to the change in Mass times the speed of light times itself. In essence matter and energy are basically the same thing, in different states, in the same equation. Only the speed of light is constant.

> A mind
> once stretched,
> never goes back to
> its original size.

Taken a step further when one approaches and arrives at the speed of light squared then energy and mass divided into each other become a singularity – at one with the universe. They are everywhere in the singularity we know as the cosmos.

This is a scientific approach to trying to explain the thinking behind the various mystical systems of divination such as astrology, palmistry and numerology.

Science and mysticism have as an underlying root; the idea of the oneness, or should I say wholeness of the universe.

Life is a form of energy. Love is the ultimate form of energy, more like a glue, that holds it all together. It adds light unto our lives.

Now let's have some fun and take a leap of faith as do

all explorers. Ask yourself this question: If everything is part of the whole universe by the fact it is part of the family we call energy, then is it possible that we haven't fully uncovered the truth behind these ancient systems of scientific inquiry, called astrology, palmistry and numerology? Maybe there is a hidden power, just beyond our awareness, in the signs of the zodiac and these early attempts at scientific explanation?

An 'Ah-Ha!' story

THE STARFISH

The storm left the beach covered in debris. I walked around the thousands of starfish the storm waves had thrown onto the beach. In the distance, I spotted an old man grasping something in his hand and flinging it back into the ocean. He repeated the ritual over and over again.

"Good evening," I said as I approached the gray haired gentleman. "What are you doing?"

"I'm throwing the dying starfish back into the sea. Otherwise, they'll die," he replied.

"Old man, why waste your time. They'll die sooner or later, anyhow," I said. "This beach is miles long. What you're doing won't make a difference."

> When an atom vibrates, the universe shakes

"I hear you son," he said. "Thanks for sharing your thoughts."

My job done, I continued on my way leaving the old man to himself. The wind whispered at my back beckoning at me to turn. Once again, I saw the old man bending down. He picked up another starfish and flung it into the sea. The wind carried his words to me. "Made a difference to that one."

Discover… All things are not as they seem…
Each moment of every day is a new beginning…
Life is the ultimate learning experience.

Comes the Dawn

After a while you learn
the subtle difference
between holding a hand
and chaining a soul.
And you learn
that love doesn't mean leaning
and company doesn't mean security
And you begin to learn
that kisses aren't contracts
and presents aren't promises.
And you begin to accept your defeats
With your head up and your eyes ahead
with the grace of a woman
not the grief of a child.
And you learn to build all your bridges on today
because tomorrow's ground is
too uncertain for plans.
And futures have a way of falling down
in mid-flight.
And after a while, you learn
that sunshine burns you if you get too much,
so plant your own garden
and decorate your own soul,
Instead of waiting for someone to bring you flowers.
And you learn
that you really can endure,
that you really are strong
And you really do have worth.
And you learn
and you learn
with every good-bye
you learn….

Anonymous
Written on the walls in a women's prison

U nusual Fact and
A wonderful uncommon act of kindness

An impoverished 96 year old woman, in Cleveland, was swindled out of $76,000 by a crooked lawyer. The jurors at the lawyer's trial gave him a 10 year prison term. The best part is seven jurors set up a trust fund to help the victim.

B eing driven crazy by what someone is doing?

Have a problem dealing with them? Here's a great technique for resolving these minor irritations before they become BIG. Try this fill in the blanks approach.

I feel _____ (label your feeling)
When you _____ (describe the annoying behavior)
Please _____ (suggest a suitable replacement behavior which is acceptable to you)

Here are a couple of examples...

I feel upset when you yell at me. Please lower your voice.

I feel frustrated when you leave your clothes lying on the couch. Please put them in the clothes hamper.

> There are only two things you can control,
> your own thoughts and actions.

What makes this very effective is that you aren't using blame, guilt or other negative emotional statements. The importance is that you take ownership of your feelings and become aware of them. Objectively state what behavior you do not want and most importantly give a positive suggestion of acceptable behavior to replace that which bothered you. Practice this, and you'll be amazed how those around you will start to slowly deal with situations that may have become battle zones.

Be embraced — Share this neat little poem

Hugs....

It's wondrous what a hug can do
A hug can cheer you when you're blue
A hug can say "I love you so" or
"Gee, I hate to see you go."
A hug is "welcome back again" and
"Great to see you!" "Where've you been?"
A hug can soothe a small child's pain
And bring a rainbow after rain.
The Hug! There's no doubt about it
We scarcely could survive without it.
A hug delights and warms and charms
It must be why "God" gave us arms.
Hugs are great for fathers and mothers.
Sweet for sisters, swell for brothers
And chances are your favorite aunts
Love them more than potted plants.
Kittens crave them: puppies love them
Heads of state are not above them.
A hug can break the language barrier
And make travels so much merrier.
No need to fret above your store of 'em
The more you give, the more there's more of 'em.
So stretch those arms without delay
And give someone a hug today

Author Unknown

Create a Hug Coupon

Just take a small piece of paper and write on it
Good for one hug or two or more.
Cashable anytime.
Nice part is hugs are healing, free and not taxed yet!

T o love for the sake of being loved is human,
But to love for the sake of loving is angelic.

Alphonse de Lamartine

H ealth trivia of the most important kind

When is a nut not a nut?
When it's a peanut! Officially it is a legume.
All foods are not created equal. Just because we label something, doesn't mean it is what the label says. According to Dr. George Grant, peanuts have a powerful toxin called aflatoxin.

If you are going to have a nut butter, almond butter is significantly more nutritious because it contains vitamin E and other fats essential to wellbeing and healing in nature.

> TIP: Get almond butter at a health food store or unsalted plain almonds and make your own in a blender – you'll use less and get significantly greater nutritional value for your money.

L ess is more!!!

The idea isn't unbearable for those who have embraced the movement to simplicity. Nudism might be an extreme example of this, but in reality it is about practicing thankfulness.

What ever material things you have, be thankful for them. Running water. Waking up in the morning. All your hair. A bald head – so you don't have to wash and comb your hair. One meal a day. Clean water. A teddy bear to hug and love. Quality not quantity is the call to arms. Practicing thankfulness will enrich your life. …Do it now!

Some folks say a blessing or prayer for the food they eat. Others just consume.

Silently, I take a moment to thank the life that gave of itself to nourish my body. In this way, I get a double whammy by nourishing my soul. You can too! Just do it… Even if it is for only a second of silence, be grateful and acknowledge the gifts of the Universal Intelligence – God.

Why is it…

When I was a kid, I wanted to grow up.
 Now I am a grown up, and I want to be a kid.

I have seen the shadow,
 the shadow saw me.
I have known the shadow,
 the shadow knows me.
I embraced the shadow,
 the shadow embraced me.
 I cried – my soul nearly died.
I have seen the light,
 the light sees me.
I have known the light,
 the light knows me.
I embraced the light,
 the light embraced me.
 I laughed – my soul found tranquility.
I have known the darkness of the day,
 the light of the night.
I have known what it is to be without sight.
 I found the answer – it was in me.
 Love truly helped, set me free.

An 'Ah-Ha!' story

IT COULD HAVE BEEN WORSE

Not long ago I met a grade school friend from my kindergarten days. It had been decades since we last met. We did a lot of catching up. He asked me how things are going.

"Well…" I said, "I had an accident, which left me with a partially paralyzed left side, collapsed lung, heart attack and chronic pain."

"It could have been worse," Glen said.

"You know the business I was in. It went bankrupt and I only owed the bank $10,000,000," I added.

> That which doesn't kill me,
> makes me stronger.

"It could have been worse," Glen said.

I was getting a bit frustrated. I just wanted to be heard. A dash of sympathy or empathy would've been appreciated. I decide to try one more time.

"My marriage of 17 years is coming to an end. My wife and I are getting divorced," I said, figuring this last attempt would work.

Glen looked me in the eye, and said, "It could have been worse."

"Glen, what do mean it could have been worse?" I asked in a frustrated tone.

Glen looked me straight in the eye, and said, "Ken, it could have been me."

 Only those who dare, truly live.

Ruth Freedman

Trivia of the most lovemaking kind
that pays dividends!?!

According to *Psychology Today,* "Women who read romance novels make love 74% more often than woman who do not read romance novels."

Ladies, LionHearted Publications has great romance novels, not available in bookstores. They range from historical to modern settings. The three I reviewed were great reads.

An interesting twist is that LionHearted empowers their writers by giving them a better, bigger and faster return for their labors. Empowering writers and readers is their mission.

Tip: Statistics indicate that 5% of men covertly read romance novels. The owners of LionHearted Publications believe it is now 10% and increasing. Ladies, lend the guys your romance novels. You'll add zing to your love life if you tell them that men who read them benefit from the knowledge. Guys, what a wonderful gift these would make for your partners.

Hot tip: They are located in Zephyr Cove, Nevada. In the USA and Canada to order call their toll free number 1-888-lion-hrt (546-6478) Overseas orders call 702-588-1388. Ask for their super special book package offer and how you can make money sharing the LionHearted Romance novel series. Tell them Ken Vegotsky, the author of the Make Love With Life books sent you.

> Saving you $ and helping you earn $, so you get a little more pleasure out of life, is also what Making Love With Life is about.

Thought for the day

It is in the simplest of deeds,
that the greatest of works are done.

Fortunately psychoanalysis is not the only way to
resolve inner conflict.
Life itself still remains a very effective therapist.

Karen Horney

A hundred years from now, it will not matter
what my bank account was, the sort of house
I lived in or the kind of clothes I wore. But the
world may be much different because I was important in
the life of a child.

Author Unknown

Discover a quick way to live in the moment. Try this

How to access inner peace
anywhere, anytime, anyplace…
A quick 60 second stress reduction technique:

Do this first thing in the morning before you get out of
bed, or during a meeting, before you start working or walk
back into the house. It helps you focus on the moment.

1) Decide you are going to do this… and just do it.
2) Focus on your breathing. Imagine each breath in is from
   heaven, and each breath out is going to the earth. Breath
   deeply at least three times.
3) Now, close your eyes – except if your driving.
4) In your mind say *'Inhale 1'* as you start to inhale. Hold the
   breath in your belly for a bit.
   In your mind say *'Exhale 1'* as you start to exhale. Empty
   your lungs fully before starting the next breath.
   Continue doing the same thing.
   'Inhale 2' …hold *'Exhale 2'* … *'Inhale 3'* …hold *'Exhale 3'*
   'Inhale 4' …hold *'Exhale 4'* …
5) Repeat the cycle starting at 1 again or continue counting
   upward. If a thought creeps into your mind while doing
   this, then start again at 1. The more you practice this technique the easier it becomes.

Some of the benefits are reduced heart rate, lower blood pressure but most importantly you are focusing on the moment, gently clearing the clutter of thoughts that are constantly assaulting you.

> TIP: If this counting technique isn't for you, then just repeat this sentence. "I breath in…. hold… I breath out… I breath in… hold… I breath out…. If you are worried about missing an appointment put your alarm on. Trust yourself and discover this quick and easy way to live in the moment.
> Think of this as giving yourself a tax free gift – you'll get a charge out of it.

Hypnotic Journey of Gentle Surrender, is an instructional and music filled audio that induces and helps you achieve deep relaxation. My voice and the music are blended using numerous techniques. The above is a written sample of what is recorded. To order the audio, call toll free 1-800-263-1991.

Life's sweetest joys are hidden in unsubstantial things; an April rain, a fragrance, a vision of blue wings.

Mary Riley Smith

The people who get on in this world are the people who get up and look for the circumstances they want, and if they can't find them, make them.

George Bernard Shaw

Be positive… Be life affirming… Say to yourself

I'm attracting prosperity into my life, and the lives of those around me.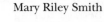

Repeat this to yourself frequently through the day. Post notes with it in places where you'll see it frequently. Time will make this become your reality. If it's to be, it's up to you!

An 'Ah-Ha!' story

PEOPLE ARE JUST LIKE COWS

by Raymond Aaron

A friend told me something he learned as a child about cows. It's a true story. Here's how he told me about it...

"My most vivid recollections of being a little boy growing up on the farm are those related to the river which flowed through our farm. I can fondly remember the fun we had splashing in the water on hot summer days. But I also remember the winters when it froze solid.

"Every winter there was one particular chore that always fell to me. I had to chop a hole through the ice in the middle of the river, open the barn and bring the cows down so that they could drink from the hole. I recall almost every winter's day reopening that hole, getting wet, getting chilled to the bone and bring out the thirsty cows. Even though it still makes me shiver, there was one bright spot.

"At the end of the first winter that it had been my chore, I remember laughing at those crazy cows. You see... as spring approached, the ice began to melt and slowly recede from the banks of the river. Those cows would wade right through the water they needed so badly and then struggle up onto the firmer ice to drink through the hole. They didn't stop this pattern until the ice broke up and the hole was carried downstream. Springtime after Springtime after Springtime those cows kept up this same routine. They never learned."

After laughing at this amusing story, I sat silently for a long time to try to discover how many ways, in my own life, I was just like those silly cows!

Raymond Aaron, a dynamic self-empowerment speaker who runs critically acclaimed Monthly Mentor™ networking groups for entrepreneurs. To find out more information about his groups call (905) 881-8995.

Be a kid again

Have a pajamas party with a bunch of friends. Use sleeping bags and camp out in your living room. Bring flashlights so you can tell ghosts stories and read in the dark.

Today do an uncommon act of kindness
Enrich another's life… just for the sake of it

Compliment someone sincerely, help someone with their load, say or do something without expecting anything in return.

Live your life each day as you would climb a mountain.
An occasional glance toward the summit keeps the goal in mind, but many beautiful scenes are to be observed from each new vantage point. Climb slowly, steadily, enjoying each passing moment, and the view from the summit will serve as fitting climax for the journey.

H. Melchert

For centuries Mankind has worked on the assumption
that we could pursue the goal of steady progress without disturbing the fundamental equilibrium of the world's atmosphere and its living system. In a very short time that comfortable assumption has been shattered."

Margaret Thatcher,
Past Prime Minister of the United Kingdom

Excess always carries its own retribution.

Ouida

 T hought provoking point to ponder.
  Freedom is a state of mind

The 'Pain-Pleasure Principle' is one of the great
tools used by manipulators as they try to lead you to their
perception of your true happiness. Advertisers are very
good at this using words such as *New, Improved, New &
Improved, Scientific Break Through, Time saver,* and so on for
products or services which seldom have much added value
over the original. Their purpose is to keep you slightly
unbalanced with a promise of incredible life enhancing
improvement. This principle forms the basis of the con-
sumer society that is dying of its own consumption.

Externalized happiness which makes happiness seem
almost attainable, often comes with a price costing you
dearly in energy, money and time. It is not the true source
of happiness. Happiness springs from within.

By using the tools of realization and awareness, you discover how and when you're being manipulated and you
can break free of this powerful cycle. Think of it as taking
a mental vaccination against the external powers of manipulation. Free yourself... Liberate yourself from the addictive nature of consumerism and the perpetual pain it
brings to those who keep striving to find externally the happiness which is waiting to be mined from within.

 T here is beauty in the forest
  When the trees are green and fair
  There is beauty in the meadow
  When wild flowers scent the air
  There is beauty in sunlight
  And the soft blue beams above.
  Oh, the world is full of beauty
  When the heart is full of love."

Author Unknown

Trivia of the most interesting kind

 ## "Matchmaker, matchmaker make me a $1,000,000 match…"

Do you want to marry a world class Mr./Ms. Right!? Do you have a friend in need? Now's your chance to do a good deed. It's FREE!

Mate-Search International charges it's rich and famous clients $10,000 for ten matches. Business tycoons, professional athletes, sheiks, movie stars, socialites, etcetera use this one of a kind service.

They found a husband for a famous movie star, a wife for a Saudi Sheik, a husband for a best selling romance novelist, a wife for a prominent law school dean – just to name a few. To date, the results are 19 marriages, 17 engagements and 18 cohabitations.

The average Joe or Josephine can get into their database-of-love for FREE! How?

Send three photos, a work resume and a biographical sketch to Robert Davies & Associates, Mate-Search International, 2024 Stone Ridge Lane, Villanova, Pennsylvania 19085. It's that simple!

TIP. Got a spare $10,000 and want to find your perfect match, call Robert at 610-527-6749.

P.S. Robert, I'm sending you a copy of this book, three photos, work resume and biography as soon as it is published. That is unless I get very lucky and/or have a spare $10,000 kicking around.

To save a little time here's a sketch of my bio:
Single – Divorced after 17 years married to a very fine lady.
Two great kids.
Birthday – December 18, 1951.
For presents I accept cash, charge cards, gifts and plain old best wishes.
Sign – Sagittarius.
Hobbies – loves walks in woods, candlelight moments, hugs and kisses, living in the moment. Loves people.

Down to earth – I don't feel the need or desire to dress up preferring to be very very comfortable.

Experimental cook – in other words my mistakes become soup.

Work – Author, professional speaker and entrepreneur alias professional mischief maker.

Income – Roller coaster style.

Physical features – Heavyset alias cuddly. Five foot six and a half inches. Left arm partially paralyzed, collapsed lung. Full head of dark brown hair with a sprinkling of gray.

Stench of humor, I'd say. Others say I have a sense of humor.

Favorite hobby – Making Love With Life!

U se this key to success

    Try out your ideas by visualizing them in action.

David Seabury

T he dreamers are the saviors of the world.

James Allen, 1864-1912,
world renowned English poet and writer.

This quote is from his classic book on positive thinking and personal growth, *As A Man Thinketh*. It is also available in an edition titled *As A Woman Thinketh*.

Give yourself, family, friends and children these books as gifts. I gave a copy to my daughter and one to my son to read and cherish when I am long gone. Inside, I marked off passages that resonate in harmony with my inner being. It's part of my legacy for them. The books are short, easy to read, beautiful classics sharing enlightenment and happiness.

> Tend the garden
> of your soul

A secret for a stress free working and adult life is found in this saying:

Do what you love and love what you do.

Alternative health trivia of the most important kind

Discover a natural way to help reduce painful menstruation and the effects of menopause or morning sickness.

Homeopathy is one of the gentlest and safest forms of medical intervention. It is the first line of medical intervention in many European and other countries.

Sepia, a dried ink secretion of the Cuttlefish found near the Atlantic Ocean end of Mediterranean Sea and in the North Sea is one of the oldest gynecological remedies with no known side effects.

This is according to Dr. A. Vogel's *Swiss Guide to Homeopathic Medicines.* A. Vogel, a Swiss pioneer of natural choices since the early 1900's, uses modern pharmaceutical production facilities and the finest ingredients in Switzerland. Their high quality natural products are available worldwide.

I perceive us to be spiritual beings. The human experience is the garden of our souls.

Laughter — of the healing kind

Start your day in a new way.
Look at yourself in the mirror and have a good laugh.

P.S. I see myself as a well disguised Robert Redford… Of course there are a few minor differences… Okay! Okay, it's a great disguise I'm wearing.

Point to ponder

Do not allow yourself to become upset by people or things. They are powerless. Your reaction is their power.

Anonymous

Renew and reaffirm a relationship with this lovely poem

Now you feel no Rain,
for each of you will be shelter for the other.
Now you will feel no cold,
for each of you will be warmth for the other.
Now there is no more loneliness,
for each of you will be companion to the other.
Now you are two persons,
but there is only one life before you.
Go now to your dwelling,
to enter into the days of your life together.
And may your days be good, and long upon the earth.

American Indian Wedding Prayer

Enrich your life

Don't read the newspaper or watch the news on TV
for a day, a week or longer.
It soothes the mind.

Each of us is recognized by the brilliance of our light.

Alice Bailey

An unusual gift of love

Acknowledge a friend, spouse, child, relative or someone special in your life. Make a list of their positive qualities. Now put it in a letter or record it onto an audiotape to give to them as a surprise gift. They'll treasure it forever.

Acknowledging another is a beautiful gift. It is the little things that make a big difference.

Ken Vegotsky

Be a kid again

Chase a cloud. Fly a kite.
Daydream.

An 'Ah-Ha!' story

THE WHOLE PICTURE

Three blind men were asked to describe what an elephant is like.

Each one was given a different spot to touch. One by the trunk. One by a leg. One by the tail.

They were given a few minutes to examine their spot.

Not all things are as they seem.
Use all your senses to the fullest.
They are a gift.

"Elephants are like snakes," said the first one who explored the trunk.

"Elephant are like trees," said the second one, whose arms were wrapped around the elephants legs.

"Elephants are like brushes," said the third blind man, as he waved the tail in the air.

Ponder this

Take the pooh-pooh of your past,
make it into fertilizer for your present,
so you can grow a new tomorrow today.

Be a kid again

Have a belly laughing session.

<u>Equipment</u> – Three or more willing participants.
The more, the merrier.

<u>Method</u> – Lie on your back. Rest your head on someone else's belly. Create a closed loop, a circle of participants, until everyone has a head on their belly. Choose a starter. They laugh once. Ha! Then continue in a clockwise fashion, the next person laughs twice. Ha! Ha! The next one goes Ha! Ha! Ha! You keep adding a laugh a person until that moment when laughter embraces everyone. Don't stop… just enjoy.

Here are some of the benefits. Laughter has incredible curative properties – your body produces healing chemistry. It's tax free. It's not fattening. You find out who your friends are. It's great! In some of my seminars, I have seen adults reconnect to their inner child just by doing this.

I created an audio tape of a babbling brook with my children's laughter just for this reason. I call it *The Gift of Laughter*. On side two of the tape is a gentle musical and word audio for relaxation. It's infectious, healthy and inexpensive fun. To order see the back of book for special offer.

Laughter's power is so strong that cancer departments in some hospitals have laugh therapy sessions. This idea is based on the work of Norman Cousins who was diagnosed as terminally ill from cancer.

His doctor's expectation was that he wouldn't live many more months. He challenged the negative prognosis by using the power of the mind combined with the bodies natural wisdom to heal itself. How? He isolated himself from the outside world, rented classic comedy films and laughed his way to wellness. Laughter plus nutritional supplements cured his cancer. He lived decades beyond the doctors prognosis. Discover his wonderful life affirming laugh therapy in his book, *Anatomy of An Illness*.

Whatever is flexible and flowing will continue to grow; whatever is rigid will tend to die.

Tao Te Ching

Give without remembering.
Receive without forgetting.

Not so Zen ancient Oriental saying

Today's philosophy, becomes tomorrow's common sense.
Chinese fortune cookie saying.

I found my guru.
He was staring back at me from the mirror.

Cheap trip

Travel the world and have an incredible experience without leaving the comfort of your seat.

Do you want to feel connected with humanity? Get a copy of this incredible video. Better yet, see it at a theater near you.

Baraka, from Astral Video, is a movie without words. The Earth's glories are captured in a spellbinding display of humanities diversity and impact upon the planet. It transcends language barriers and geographical locations. The movie, photographed on six continents and in 24 countries, has an awesome mix of visuals and music.

I was inspired and living fully in the moment during the show. *Baraka* is destined to become a timeless underground classic.

> TIP: Ask your local movie house to get it. I loved it so much I bought a video copy. Unfortunately the TV screen does not do it justice.

Share the experience. You'll be glad you did.

Love affirming thought for today

Lord, make me an instrument of thy peace.
>   Where there is hatred... let me sow love.
>   Where there is injury... pardon.
>   Where there is doubt... faith.
>   Where there is despair... hope.
>   Where there is darkness... light.
>   Where there is sadness... joy.

O Divine Master, grant that I may not so much seek
>   To be consoled... as to console.
>   To be understood... as to understand,
>   To be loved... as to love.

For
>   It is in giving... that we receive.
>   It is in pardoning... that we are pardoned.
>   It is in dying... that we are born to eternal life.

Saint Francis Assiss

Do this today... Renew an old acquaintance

Mail them a note saying you'd like to get together with them and the drink and dessert is your treat. To heighten the fun, put half of a five dollar bill with the letter – that way they'll know you're serious.

I wrote this for my daughter one weekend when she was staying with me

> **Your laughter is like fireworks,**
> **It adds a burst of color to my day.**
> **When you leave,**
> **it's like the night sky after the fireworks —**
> **awesome and missing something beautiful —**
> **YOU**

I put it in my Apple computer and ran off a copy on a sheet of beautiful sunset paper from Geopaper™ by Geographics. Now she has it, with a collection of sayings I created for her, on her bedroom wall in her mom's home. I did the same for my son – adding my phone number to let them know they can call me anytime they want to.

My children are my inspiration. They inspired many of my sayings you are now reading.

> TIP: If you cannot find the specialty paper in your local Staples, The Office Place, Business Depot or stationery supplier call Geographics head office in Blaine, Washington at (360) 332-6711.

Making Love With Life
Gifts from the heart – under a buck!

Create inexpensive mini-posters for gift and special occasion giving. To test out the idea, here's what you do if you don't have a computer and printer.

1) Use the saying above. Cover up all the words on this page that are not relevant.

2) Set the photocopier to an enlargement setting that will make the saying almost fill a sheet of paper. Use plain white paper to test.

3) Take the Geopaper with the sunset on it, or any speciality paper that suits your fancy and copy the enlarged saying onto it.

4) Add a touch of class. Give it your personal touch by signing your name.

5) Roll up the mini-poster, white side facing out, and put a small ribbon around it.

Voila! A beautiful, customized gift of gratitude and love for someone special in your life.

> TIP: I put many inspirational sayings on these sheets for gifts and for myself. Now, to help me through my day, inspiring thoughts plaster my home and office walls.

Eight keys for achieving a happier life

1) Be flexible. There is no single approach that works for everyone.

2) Many possible solutions exit for any situation.

3) The problem and solution may not be related.

4) The best approach is usually the simplest and least invasive.

5) People can and do get better quickly.

6) Change happens constantly.

7) Focus on your resources and strengths, not your weaknesses and deficits.

8) Let go of the past by focusing on the future.

Focus on these three aspects – solutions, changing your attitudes and positive actions leading to positive outcomes. This is the core of Rational-Emotive Therapy and numerous other books that say to feel good think positive and do positive.

Trivia of the most interesting kind

Timing is everything when tapping into the female love cycle. A woman's sex drive is primarily powered by minute amounts of testosterone and related adrogens (male hormones) which are released around the time of ovulation. The adrenal glands and ovaries produce these love chemicals. Studies indicate that this is when most women's sex drives peak.

The levels of these love chemicals are significantly higher in males which is why men seem always to be ready for a sexual encounter.

Aging and menopause sometimes will cause a physical reversal of these chemicals levels in the female and male. Maybe this is one reason why older women should marry younger men and vice-versa?

Excerpt from *For Lovers Only: 222 Ways to Enhance the Magic & Make Love With Life* by Ken Vegotsky, AGES Publications

Humorous insight

To forge a dream takes tender loving care, luck,
tenacity and a heck of a lot of stupidity.
The results are worth it.

The secret of a life of prosperity is found in the *Law of Manifestation...* Simply put

What you think, believe and act upon is what happens.

Enrich your life now

Take a minute to remember a happy occasion in your life... a smiling moment. Now, just do it — Be Happy!

Galling health tip, so to speak

Extra virgin olive oil has been discovered to have life affirming properties. It helps the body use its natural abilities to heal itself.

> TIP: Have gallstone problems... Here's an ancient remedy that works for many. It may even save you the cost of expensive surgery and all the potential hazards of surgery. Speak to your doctor about what you plan to do.
> Use 1 quart or litre of extra virgin olive with freshly squeezed lemons to help rid your body of the gallstones.
> Here's how: In the early evening, take two tablespoons of freshly squeezed lemon juice, then a 1/4 of a cup (4 tablespoons) of extra virgin olive oil, every fifteen minutes. Repeat this until you finish the bottle of olive oil.
> Lie down on your right side and go to sleep.

During the night this softens the gallstones and you will start passing them in your bowels movements. Nature supplies us with healing processes that evolved over thousands of generations of human development. The plant and human partnership go way back, long before the recent invention of what is called the pharmacological based medicine, in this century.

Body parts are there for a reason, be cautious about giving up parts that the universe saw fit to give you.

Have a mental health breakfast... Start your day with this thought

I wake up in the morning, that's enough for me.
The rest of the day is a bonus.

The greatest gift we can give one another is rapt attention to one another's existence.

Sue Ebaugh

I know what I have to be doing. Why aren't I doin' it?

Roger Farguson

W hy is it...

When I was a kid,
princesses and princes lived happily ever after.
Now I am grown up and they live happily ever after,
but not with each other.

T hought provoking idea

Time is an illusion. The past, present and future are all one. It is only the mind which tricks us into believing otherwise. One way to discover this truth is to create time capsules. Here's how:

Just before my first child was born, I started saving interesting newspaper clippings and other small paraphernalia of life that I thought might interest her when she had grown up. Clear plastic bags were stuffed with items like her first hair clippings, shoes, and the headline of the newspaper the day she was born – Princess Stephanie of Monaco had been involved in some event. Incidentally my daughters name is Stephanie.

> Time is an illusion.
> All is in the now.

Through the years, I collected things and culled them out once the clear plastic bag got too full. Then I would label and date them, and use a straw to suck out the air before sealing the bag. Then I'd put it in another bag.

Today my children's first few years of life sit on a bookshelf along side one I did about my life at that time. They wait patiently for enough linear time to pass so that the past can be brought into the present, which is sometime in the future. Fact is that time is here already, if you realize I could see far enough ahead to know that this is so.

Discover the medicine cabinet for life – Nature

Extra virgin olive oil refers to the first pressing of the olives before using or adding any chemicals. It appears to have therapeutic value.

Studies of Mediterranean people indicate they have greatly lower levels of heart disease in spite of a propensity to being overweight. What is amazing is the olive plant's power to reduce blood pressure and incidence of heart disease, and to heal viral and bacterial infections where other medications have failed. Scientists recently discovered it is packed with phytochemicals that have incredible healing powers. What is astounding is that the Bible and historical documents throughout recorded history have mentioned this. The olive leaves contain oleuropein which has powerful disease-resisting properties. While many of the properties of the olive tree are allegorical, scientists are proving nature's incredible therapeutic and curative properties.

The 9 1/2 Laws of Laziness

Law of Laziness 1.
Formerly called Law of Stupidity 8.8
– Do it once. Do it right.
I didn't want to make another list,
so I put it in the Laws of Stupidity list..

Law of Laziness 2.
– When you want to complain, don't!
Let someone else do it for you.

Law of Laziness 3.
– Write your own Laws of Laziness,
I'm going for a break.

Law of Laziness 9 1/2.
– Go back to Law of Laziness #1
This is the lazy way of getting out of creating
a whole list of Laws. Now it's your turn.

Trivia of the most important kind

When is a healthy oil not what it appears to be — when it is canola oil. Rapeseed, the source plant for canola oil, was originally used for purposes such as pesticides and insecticides.

In the 1950's, irradiation was used on the rapeseed to transform its chemical composition so it could become an edible food product. In its original state, it is toxic to human and animal life. Mechanical and chemical processing removes the toxicity, yet does not add the healthy benefits derived from oils such as extra virgin olive oil. Marketing research indicated that canola oil would be more digestible to the public than any term with the word rape in it.

When is an oil not what it appears to be?

When it is relabeled.

Be a kid again

Have a Double Bubble Gum Chewing Contest.

Here's what you do...

Buy a bucket of your favorite bubble gum. I prefer regular flavor Bazooka or Double Bubble. Insert one piece at a time and chew until softened. Then another piece... and another... and another... and another... By now you get the idea. Keep on going until your jaw's tired out, preferably before your teeth or caps fall out.

Now comes the fun part. The winner is the one who doesn't have a locked jaw when all is said and chewed, so to speak. The victory celebration is the winner gets to blow a big bubble.

Tip — Increase the fun quotient... Do it with a kid.

My seven year old son, Alan, and I were out for a drive.

I challenged him to a bubble gum eating contest.

"Sure, Dad," he said, as he starting unwrapping the first of many bubble gums. Testosterone challenges start early in life for little boys. One… chew… two… chew… three… chew… Around twelve pieces, a muffled voice spoke out.

"Dad, I can't chew any more pieces. Anyway, it's not fair, you've got a bigger mouth."

By this time, I was ahead by at least eight more pieces.

"Dad, to be the official winner you got to blow your bubble now," Alan said.

Testosterone challenges continue in big boys called Dad also. I proceeded to blow the biggest, hugest, most humungous bubble. It got so big that I pulled the car over and took off my glasses.

> If spot reducing really worked, then people who chew bubble gum would have very thin faces.

Out of the corner of my eye, I saw this little index finger advancing. In the background, a gloating, smiling face bobbed with a sparkling set of eyes. I'd been set up by a master bubble gummer. My bubble burst as his laughter danced in the air.

Alan was, is and always will be the undisputed master of bubble gum chewers and gentle pranks. I'm just the biggest kid – again.

Incidentally, I'm not related to any dentist, nor do I receive any commission for this suggestion.

Health care with a twist

Ancient Chinese doctors got paid to keep their patients healthy. Pro-actively, doctors helped nurture their patient's wellbeing. If the person became ill, the doctor had to treat them for free until they were well again.

Ken Vegotsky

An 'Ah-Ha!' Story

MY VISA AND BUICK ARE HAVING AN AFFAIR

There was a time when I was starting my businesses that I barely had enough to pay the rent, for that matter, to even put food on the table.

For over three years, I'd been digging deeply into my savings – very deeply. My fourteen year old General Motors car kept calling out for attention. Unfortunately, I didn't have much of a choice. I needed it to do my work, but could not afford to replace it.

That's when I discovered how charitable people you support with loyalty can be – especially those who had experienced hard times. Here's what happened.

> What comes around, goes around
> – in life, in business, in all we do.
> This is also known as loyalty.

Eight years ago, Mike opened up a One Stop Auto garage. Since that day, I have been a customer of his. One day, we were talking about the difficult business environment of the least decade. The recession seemed to never end, and when it did, those folks in the private sector were not the ones who seemed to benefit the most.

"Mike, don't forget to tell your bankers, I'm a major source of your cash flow. They can bank on it," I kidded him. Lines of credit were what kept most business alive and operating.

My six year old General Motors car had matured into a fourteen year old. A testimony as much to the solid workmanship of an American made car as it is to Mike.

A dash of TLC, loads of cash and the magic of Mike's

mechanics kept it going. I believe chewing gum is what kept the trim on.

Our relationship is like a marriage, lots of ups and downs especially on the hoist. At times, I want to divorce myself from the Buick, but find it hard to since it costs me less than a thousand a year to keep it going – including the time I put a used rebuilt transmission in the car.

I believe my Visa and Buick were having an affair. Well, the day before Christmas, my Buick put up one heck of a fuss. It was just past noon and every one was closing their business that day. Fighting and screaming as cars are want to do, I miraculously made it to Mike's. He was closed.

I honked and he opened the garage door. With every bit of strength left in her, the Buick made it into the warmth of the garage and died. Smoke and fumes billowed from the engine and into the passenger compartment.

A quick check found the problem – unfortunately every parts supply and other business had closed for Christmas.

With luck, used parts scavenged from the garbage bin and two hours of labor, my car was up and running.

I offered to pay Mike and the mechanic. He refused any money. With a wave and good cheer he sent me on my way. As I drove, I swore I heard a Ho! Ho! Ho! in the distance.

Practice this

TLC — Tender Loving Care
expanded to
STLC — Self-Tender Loving Care

Why is it…

When I was a kid,
grandma made the best food.
Now that I am grown up,
my doctor says don't eat it anymore.
Is that what they mean when they say, food for thought?!

Ancient wisdom with a modern day twist

LESS IS MORE is the realization that quality, not quantity, is a key to a happy life. The interesting part is that quality does not have to be measured in materialistic terms, but more so is defined as a state of being.

Happiness can be seen as externally generated – more possessions, more food, fancy clothes, etc... Whereas bliss is an internally generated state. When living in bliss, you can enter into *satori* – a supreme state of being.

Nothing in the world can take the place of persistence.
Talent will not: nothing is more common than
                    unsuccessful men with talent.
Genius will not: unrewarded genius is
                  almost a proverb.
Education will not: the world is full of educated derelicts.
Persistence and determination are omnipotent.
Calvin Coolidge

Life is either a daring adventure or nothing at all.
Helen Keller

Health trivia of the most important kind

Garlic power to the rescue... Garlic, to grow, needs and stores selenium. This trace mineral appears to decrease one's odds of getting certain cancers. It also increases the benefits of vitamin E.

Take vitamin E in as close to a natural state as possible since this is less stressing to the liver. It appears to have profound benefits to the heart and other body parts.

Capture a dream tonight

Native Americans use Dream Catchers to help them get a sound and good nights sleep. Here's an approach I use. It doesn't cost a cent and it works.

Just before you fall asleep, in your minds eye weave a round web with a hole in the middle. Picture a giant feather hanging from the bottom.

Slowly breath in and out. Imagine that all the good dreams are coming in through hole and all the bad dreams are getting caught in the web you wove. Know this... the morning sun melts all the bad dreams and they flow away through the feather.

Just before you fall asleep, smile and imagine yourself waking up in the morning with a renewed sense of vigor and vitality.

An 'Ah-Ha!' story

THE BIG PURCHASE

Sam lost his job, home and all his material possessions.

All he had left were his wife and children – the greatest and best of treasures. It was a struggle to shelter, cloth and feed his family – yet somehow he managed to scrape enough together each day.

Unfortunately, his youngest child, Ali, became deathly ill. Sam could not afford the medicine the child needed. Finally in desperation he went to church and prayed to God to help him win the lottery. Days past, and nothing happened. Sam went back and prayed more. Weeks passed and nothing happened.

> Get involved in life to be a winner in the lottery of life.

Sam, in desperation, went back again asking God to make him a lottery winner.

Tears streamed down Sam's face as he prayed for divine intervention. Anger swelled up inside him. He yelled. He begged. Yet nothing happened.

Hours latter, as he started to leave the Church, a voice from the heavens said, "You've got to buy a ticket."

Love is an exploding cigar we willingly smoke.

Lynda Barry

Hot tip... Become a not so secret agent

Achieve a better understanding of what makes the opposite sex tick.

For women... read current issues of men's magazines such as *Men's Health* and *Playboy* – just ignore the pictures and read the articles. They'll give you insight into what men are about at this moment.

For men... read current issues of women's magazines such as *Cosmopolitan, New Women, Glamour, Mademoiselle, Maria Claire, Self, Chatelaine, Modern Women, Playgirl* – just ignore the pictures and read the articles. They'll give you insight into what women are about at this time.

TIP: Save a fortune, go to your library and browse the magazines, or borrow a few from a friend of the opposite sex. It will be quite an eye opener.

GREAT GIFT IDEA: If you like the type of information or ideas a particular magazine shares, then buy your partner a gift subscription. This way you are gently helping their perceptions of the world become more fully complete.

Excerpt from *For Lovers Only: 222 Ways to Enhance the Magic & Make Love With Life,* AGES Publications.

Why is it...

When I was a kid,
being gay meant having a good time.
Now that I am older,
being gay means an *alternative lifestyle!?*

What exactly is an alternative lifestyle anyhow?!

Our greatest glory is not in never failing,
but in rising every time we fail.

Confucius

Turn negative situations into a positive outcomes

How? Treat them as learning experiences. Detach yourself from the negative feelings and thoughts and look for positive ideas.

Put another way – Take the pooh-pooh of your past, make it into fertilizer for your present, so you can grow a new tomorrow today.

Akey to success is to turn your negatives into positives.

Ponder this problem solving technique

How do you eat an elephant?
Answer: One bite a time.

Vegetarians may choose to ask –
How do you eat a watermelon?
Answer: One bite at a time.

Ken Vegotsky

I do the very best I know how, the very best I can, and I mean to keep on doing it to the end.

If the end brings me out all right, what is said against me will not amount to anything.

If the end brings me out all wrong, ten angels swearing I was right would make no difference.

Abraham Lincoln

Back by popular demand: but this time all in one place!

The 9 ½ Laws of Stupidity?

Law of Stupidity #1
   If you don't know you can't do it – just do it!

Law of Stupidity #1.1
   There ain't no substitute for the type of stupidity I've got. Some people call it tenacity

Law of Stupidity #2
   The only stupid question, is the one not asked...
   Get what I mean?

Law of Stupidity #2.1
   ?

Law of Stupidity # 2.9
   Make Love With Life.
   If you do it right, you don't need protection.

Law of Stupidity #3
   Stupid is as stupid does. Make stupid mistakes repeatedly, until you're ready to get it right.

Law of Stupidity #4
   When something needs getting done, who do you hire? Hire yourself and don't give up!
   P.S. Remember to fire yourself at the appropriate time.

Law of Stupidity # 4.4
   If your team is losing, cheer for the other side....
   It's safer that way.

Law of Stupidity # 4.7

Giving people what they want, is easier then getting them to want what you have to give.

Law of Stupidity #5

Stupid people laugh at themselves.

Really very stupid people are the smartest of all, they laugh even harder at themselves.

Law of Stupidity #5.1

No is the best shortcut to a yes. You've just got to remember to accept it and get on with life.

Law of Stupidity # 5 $\frac{1}{5}$

Spellin' don't matter, if you don't want anybody to understood you. Neither does con text.

P.S.   I trust my computer to check spelling and make shore every word is write.

Law of Stupidity #5.7

If all else fails – your calculator breaks!? Your computer gets a glitch!? Don't worry. Count on your fingers. It works for me.

Law of Stupidity #6

If you are what you eat, and want to get healthier, become a vegetarian. If we are what we eat, does that make me a vegetable? No! I'm not a couch potato. To heal my damaged heart, that's one thing I did.

Law of Stupidity #7

Nature has great healing power. To get back to nature, take a long walk off a short peer. Just remember to put on your life preserver – first!

Law of Stupidity #8

If your memory is a problem, that's okay. Make up your own laws of stupidity. No one's gonna know the difference anyhow.

Law of Stupidity #8.3

Age is an illusion.

For example… I finally realized my Mom can't be 39

years old anymore, once I turned 40… but the pace of scientific innovation may change that cherished idea.

Law of Laziness #8.8
Do it once, do it right.

I didn't want to make another list, so I put it here.
Now renamed Law of Laziness 1.

Law of Stupidity #9 $^1/_2$
Go back to the Law of Stupidity #1.

— THE END —

Not quite yet, now create your own list of Laws of Stupidity. If you have some good ones, feel free to send them into me. Please put what it is on lower left corner of the envelope Law of Stupidity, Law of Laziness, Ah-ha story. Maximum one or two pages, typed and double spaced. Include your mailing address. If the information is used and you're the first to submit it, you'll get acknowledged in the book… sorry no money.

The lazy mans ways to write another book – more importantly to help others be of service to humanity.

No space
No time
Separate
Two Souls
Forever joined
in Universal Love

Sharon Warren
from *One Light One Love*

Read the italicized sentence. Then close the book for ten seconds and do what it asks you to do.

Don't think of pink elephants.

Times up! What were you thinking about?
Pink elephants by any chance!?
The Magical Power of the Mind™ is a presentation I love sharing. One key point is that the human mind works in **not** so mysterious ways.

Research by Marcus Conyer and other top neural-linguistic programming specialists indicates the mind interprets negative commands in a positive way — not the way they are given or meant to be received.

Recent changes to the Don't Drink and Drive advertising campaigns use this knowledge. Before, the subliminal message the mind understood was – Drink and Drive. Now they advertise **Stay Sober.**

The foundations of science are the same way. Positive results are proof. Use this information and enhance your life. Take a positive outlook on making love with life.

 I look in the mirror through the eyes of
the child that was me.

Judy Collins

A n 'Ah-Ha!' story

THE JOURNEY

I t was a day of pilgrimage to the top of a sacred mountain in India. An American tourist decided to share the experience and joined the thousands of folks taking the steep path to the mountain top.

He believed he was in excellent shape from years of jogging and exercising. Vigorously he attacked the task at hand. Half an hour later, he was out of breath and could hardly climb another step. Meanwhile, frail old men with canes and women carrying babies easily moved past him.

"I don't understand this," he said to an Indian companion. "How can they do it when I can't?"

"It is because of your typical American attitude," his friend replied. "You see everything as a challenge... a test.

You see the mountain as your enemy… one you set out to defeat. Naturally, the mountain fights back. It is stronger then you are. We don't see this sacred mountain as our enemy to be conquered. Our purpose, in the climb, is to be one with the mountain. In partnership, it lifts us up and carries us along to the top."

Doing the Waltz of Intimacy

The battle of the sexes is more about the differing styles of communications women and men have. If a man comes onto a woman, without invitation, he is seen as aggressive. If it is in response to subtle and sometimes not so subtle signals from the woman, then it is more acceptable.

Recognizing the flirting signals a woman sends, puts a new perspective on the elegance of what I call the Waltz of Intimacy. More importantly once women are aware of these signaling techniques, they can better communicate their desires without fear of rejection. This assumes the man is aware of them as well. In both cases, these rituals of mating have evolved over centuries of socialization.

Each generation builds upon the foundation of the social skills of the prior one. Understandably, these signals reduce the pain of rejection. Still, they can create a lot of frustration. Personally, I prefer directness, yet that is not necessarily the way of the world.

Here are the top ten flirting signals women make according to relationship expert, Dr. Monica Moore:

1. Eyebrow flashing, an exaggerated raising of eyebrows, of both eyes, for a couple of seconds, followed by a rapid lowering to the normal position. Usually it's combined with a smile and eye contact.

2. The lip lick, wetting a lip or both lips.

3. Short darting glances, usually occur in bouts with an average of three glances per bout.

4. The hair flip, she pushes her fingers through her hair.

5. Smiling coyly, sort of a half-smile showing little if any teeth in combination with a downward gaze or brief eye contact.

6. She bends over and whispers to a girlfriend.

7. Primping, patting or smoothing clothes even though there is no reason to.

8. Flashing a bit more leg, teasingly raises her skirt slightly.

9. She fondles keys, toys with stuff on the table or slides her hand up and down a glass.

10. She moves her body in a chair to the rhythm of music. This solitary dance is a gentle invitation to begin the Waltz of Intimacy. Go to it.

TIP: This is some of the fascinating information available in *Sex: A Man's Guide* by Stefan Betchel, Laurance Stains, and the editors of Men's Health books.

Ladies if you want to understand men better, then get a copy. You'll discover what men are being told about love and sex. Use it to gently communicate areas for growth with your male partner. Helping them is helping yourself.

Men, it's filled with pointers that can enhance your love making and intimacy abilities significantly. Being in a continuous state of self-improvement adds quality to your life and that of those around you.

 Understanding is best achieved when you start with an open mind and heart.

Why is it...

When I was a teenager,
we dreamed of a man on the moon.
Now that I am older,
we are still waiting for the first woman to get there.

Laughter is music for your ears

Make a recording of children playing and laughing. Have fun. Play it to help reconnect to your inner child or if you need a quick pick me up.

TIP: Too embarrassed to do it, then take a peak at the back of this book for ordering information, and get the audio tape *The Gift of Laughter.*

Food for thought

Consciousness is not a destination at which we finally arrive. It is an ongoing, ever-deepening,
infinitely expanding process,
a journey that perhaps has not an end.

Shakti Gawain

First aid for the male lover in your life
How to become a great lover with your lady

According to David Schnarch, Ph.D., author of *Constructing the Sexual Crucible: An Integration of Sexual and Marital Therapy,* the trick is for men to not focus on technique but on being more intimate with their partners. How men can make lovemaking more intense according to Schnarch is by understanding these points.

Woman do not show more eroticism than they think a man can handle. They've learned from experience that a woman's sexual prowess is intimidating for some men, and they hold back.

The man should gently let the woman know he is not one of those guys. Then the lady in your life may feel safe enough to share in ways he has never dreamed. This helps build a stronger bond of trust.

Start your lovemaking with an open mind. It is hard enough for a man to be expert on his own body, let alone be an expert on the female anatomy.

Deciding in advance what a woman likes predetermines your technique. According to Schnarch, "Focus on your partner and what she likes, and the technique will take care of itself."

Have an eye opener of an experience

Many men close their eyes to focus on the physical sensations of lovemaking. This shuts them off from their partners. Next time look into your partners eyes. It will not take away from the physical pleasure, but it will make the experience more intimate.

An 'Ah-Ha!' story

"Ken, could you please share what happened to me, today?" she asked. "I want others to know."

"Sure," I replied and that's how this 'Ah-Ha!' story came to be told.

THE ELEVATOR

The overcast gray sky combined with two years of frustratingly hard work starting my new business had left me with a case of the morning blahs. Being self-employed and working from home had created a feeling of isolation. Add to this a dash of holidays and the lack of a significant other in my life and you have a combination for feeling sorry for yourself.

Fortunately I've learned to tune into my emotional landscape and started dealing with my feelings.

First I tried a three minute relaxation technique to clear my mind. It did not work.

Next, I tried inhaling essential oil of lemon which usually picks me up. It did not work.

> Nothing happens by chance.

Finally, I realized I needed a break from the piles of work. So, I decided to go for a walk.

Minutes later, I was in the elevator heading outdoors. On the tenth floor, Janice, a neighbor in my building got onto the elevator.

"You look great," I said, "You've lost a lot of weight."

She looked me in the eye and said, "Yes, they discovered I had pancreatic cancer and the doctors have been doing what they can."

"Is it okay now?" I asked.

"There doesn't seem to be anything more they can do, my times almost up," she replied, "but I'm pretty lucky. I've had a great Christmas. I'll live to see the New Year and I'll savor every moment. Isn't that what it is all about!"

Gain perspective today.
    Discover that the power is within you

"How many psychiatrists or psychotherapists does it take to change a light bulb?" a friend asked.

"I don't know," I replied.

"None," he said. "It must want to change."

To promote change, you have to step outside of the boundaries of your tribe or community.

    Do it gently, as Thoreau would suggest.

Ten Vows for Success

I vow not to belittle or pity myself.
I will start each day with a plan, that maps out
    my destiny.
I will live each day with enthusiasm.
I will never be disagreeable to anyone.
In all adversity I shall seek the seeds of triumph.
Whatever task I do, I will do it the best I can.
I will always throw myself wholeheartedly into
    any task I do.
I will not wait for opportunity to embrace me.
Each night I will examine what I have done that day.
Always I will pray to keep in contact with my creator.

These and many other precious ideas are found in the writings of one of America's greatest inspirational writers, Og Mandino. Get his wonderful book *The Greatest Salesman in the World.*

In a beautifully woven tale, he describes the process, then gives universally applicable answers to that question – How can I best be of service to humanity? The ideas he shares transcend the world of sales and apply to living a better, richer and more rewarding life.

> TIP: Get a copy of this book, for your children to read when
> they grow up.

Be a kid... Discover the sensual textures of food

A dessert sampler with a difference. I call it the European sampler – a 'Little-of-Each.'

The next time you and friends come to the dessert part of your meal, each of you chooses a different dessert. Prepare identical plates of small slices of every dessert on each plate.

Now the fun begins. Take turns closing your eyes and having someone put a forkful of a dessert in your mouth.

> Rediscover what it is to be a kid again tasting food for the first time

What is very important here is NOT to label what the desserts proper name is, but to describe the: Textures – what the mouth feels. Tastes – sweet, sour, bitter, salty. Smell. Richness. Sharpness of what you are tasting.

Be as descriptive as possible. Savor the simplicity and sensuousness of the moment. Move away from the desire to be right by trying to label the dessert. Labels by their very nature remove us from being in the moment and using our senses to the maximum. They dull the authenticity of an experience.

Why is it...

> When I was young, they looked at me
> and I looked at them.
> A whistle or flirtatious word would pass through my lips.
> Now I'm much older, what I look at most is
> the birds and the bees, the flowers and the trees,
> natures sweet melody most appeals to me.

Building bridges

The Middle East is a picture of conflict to the outside world. Yet, even during numerous wars and conflicts, there are those who dream of peace. They understand the seeds for a new future must be planted in the youth of today.

The Institute of Arabic Studies is one such seed planted in the early 1950's by the members of Kibbutz Givat Haviva. It's aim is to foster positive life affirming relations between Jews and Arabs.

Programs for students of all ages are offered. One example is when the Grade 11, Jewish and Arab students share an intensive three-day series of workshops in the Youth Encounter Project.

Each year they host 3,000 students. The purpose is one of discovery and appreciating the uniqueness of each other's culture, without prejudice nor judgment. Other programs are geared to Arab and Jewish university students, Israeli artists and overseas visitors.

> Our perceptions distort our reception

 Life affirming thought for today

Seek to know yourself and accept others. It is only in accepting that one can truly begin to understand another.

An 'Ah-Ha!' story

Ann, a charming, vibrant lady, relayed two amazing events in her life. I share her stories so you may grow from them.

THE GREATEST SECRET

The family doctor came to Ann's house to see her brother who was ill – house calls still being the norm in those days.

Her Mom mentioned Ann, the baby, who lay in her crib not touching the toys or mobiles above her head. The doctor examined her and found a coating over her eyes.

"There is nothing I can do," the doctor said. "She is blind."

Weeks became months, became years. One day Ann's Mom woke up to the sounds her playing with her toys. At age two, nature had done what her doctor said was not possible.

Ann grew up, got married and had children. She took them to the same family doctor her mom and she had gone to since being a baby.

The trek was a long and difficult one with two small kids on the bus downtown. She arrived to find that the doctor had been called away on an emergency. Frustrated and tired, she decided to see a new doctor closer to home.

On her first visit, the new doctor discovered that she had precancerous cervical cancer tissues. He practiced preventive medicine, so she was treated immediately.

Today, ten years later, she is cancer free.

Having positive expectations of others
leads to positive results.

 I Love to touch you... I touch to Love you."

Sharon Warren , *Angel Fingerprints*

Communications trick to make life easier

When offering someone a choice, guide them by giving them two positive choices.

Would you like me to give you
a lovemaking idea or a romantic one?

This way you are giving the other person choices, that happen to be what may also benefit you.

Well what did you choose lovemaking or romance?

Both! ...Good choice.

See it works.

Be a kid today

Make funny faces at friends and family.

Aquick attitude adjustment for those in heat! or cold!

Winter in the north country is freezing most times. Many grumble about it, especially after a freezing rain or a snowy day. Winds chill and put icicles upon nose tips. One day a friend complained.

"It's terrible," he said, "I hate winter!"

"I prefer to look at it this way," I said. "We are one day closer to spring."

Fact is, the start of winter, the shortest day in the year, is also the beginning of spring since now the days are getting longer.

If you live in a hot, super heated climate and summers are the most uncomfortable time, then think of it this way. You are getting closer to winter.

This applies in America, Canada, Australia, New Zealand, United Kingdom – I guess pretty much everywhere. Those Canuks (Canadians) have it bad in winter in their capital Ottawa. Even the ambassador for Outer Mongolia tactfully said Ottawa is really cold in the winter. Don't worry. Canadians make up for it with a *joie de vivre* – joy for life, by practicing Eskimo Kisses, for good reason.

Visit Toronto, Ontario, Canada and discover why the United Nations repeatedly says it is the worlds most ethnically diverse city, with over 200 communities that celebrate ethnic uniqueness and diversity at many events: Caravan is a multicultural community event through out the city and Caribbana is the largest celebration and parade of Afro-American Heritage in North America. Toronto is now the third largest theater center in the world. The United Nations repeatedly chooses Canada as the best country in the world to live.

Make a random phone call of love — today!

Occasionally, I call my Mom, family or friends and leave an *I Love You...* or *You're Special* message or an inspirational saying for them, on their machine – then hang up.

I like to call a friend's answering machine the day they go on a trip, leaving an *I wanted to be the first to welcome you home...* message to warm their hearts upon arrival.

P.S.   This way I don't forget and they usually call to thank me. It is always nice to know and be acknowledged by another, freely - without expectation of a reward.

P.P.S.   Many women tell me my voice has healing properties. They've even suggested I start an inspirational bed time or morning phone service, and have requested audio tapes.

– I did it for you – Get your copy of my guided relaxation tape *Hypnotic Journey of Gentle Surrender*. Discover soothing, calming and healing secrets. The incredible music for it was created by William Outlon. My gift to you... place your credit card order for this tape today call 1-800-263-1991 (overseas (519) 396-9553) and ask for free delivery, because you read about it in a *Make Love With Life* book.

Why is it...

When I was a kid, I had high arches.
Now I am grown up, the arches have fallen.
As have many other body parts... Oh well.

The rare and beautiful experiences of divine revelation are moments of special gifts. Each of us, however, lives each day with special gifts which are a part of our very being, and life is a process of discovering and developing these God-given gifts within each one of us.

Jeane Dixon

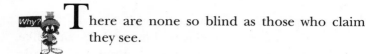 There are none so blind as those who claim they see.

I want to get excited about who you are, what you are, what you have, and what can still be for you.
I want to inspire you to see that you can go far beyond where you are right now.

Virginia Satir

Add zing to your lovemaking with an erotic mind expanding experience!

Sex therapist Bernie Zilbergeld, Ph.D., suggests a techniques he calls simmering in his book *The New Male Sexuality*. According to the ladies, this simmering technique works for them also!

Here's what you do. During the morning, when you see or hear a sexually attractive person that arouses your sexual feelings, fix the thought in your mind. Have a few moments of guilt free fantasizing about them. Replay the thought throughout the day. Return to it and relive it, an hour later. Then continue replaying it a few hours later.

Repeat. Repeat until... Here's the key – when work ends and you're on your way home, substitute your steady for the fantasy person. Keep those feelings of arousal simmering until you and your lover are ready to boil over.

> The body
> is in the mind.

Imagination used in this way is a form of directed consciousness. A simple proof that the body is in the mind.

TIP. Plan your lovemaking a day in advance. If you have kids, arrange to drop them off at a friends or babysitters for the evening, better yet overnight! Now comes the fun part. Both you and your partner consciously start simmering in the morning and cooking in the evening.

Great Spirit, Great Spirit, my grandfather,
   All over the earth the faces of living things are alike.
With tenderness have these come up out of the ground,
Look upon these faces of children without number and
with children in their arms,
that they may face the winds
and walk the good road to the day of quiet.

Black Elk, Lakota Indian Chief

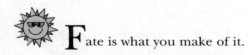 Fate is what you make of it.

Be happy — use a squabble model

According to Larry Hof, M. Div., chief operating officer at the Marriage Council of Philadelphia, the key is to resolve more arguments. Men, here are steps you can take to have a better and healthier relationship with your partner.

1. Let her vent. Move away from the idea of immediately solving the problem. This allows her to get to the underlying issues, or what is the real problem.
2. Acknowledge and take her feelings seriously. An individual's feelings are not to be judged, but rather accepted.
3. Give up the need to be right or win a victory. Search for solutions.
4. Celebrate the resolution, whether that be going out for a treat, sharing a bowl of passion fruit or going for dinner.

Try these words… "I love you and I don't want this to stand between us." says Hof.

Sixty seconds to success in Making Love With Life

Discover *The Flexible Affirmation* a focusing technique that creates positive outcomes, in your life. Tap into the power of your magical mind today.

During the depths of my recovery from a near-fatal accident, this gift from on high gave me hope to deal with intense chronic pain. Drugs didn't work. Surgery lessened it a bit. Every day the pain killed a little bit more of my mind, body and spirit. I was desperate. Desperate enough that I tried to take my own life.

This is one of the tools I unleashed for striving to survive and thrive in a world gone awry. Use this technique now. Use it until your dreams, goals or wishes come true. Frequent repetition to yourself is important.

If you desire to change a specific behavior, commit to saying it for at least 21 days. By the end of that time, you'll be amazed at the success you have with it. If you have a goal that takes a long time, then use it daily and keep repeating it in your head until it comes to pass. Here's a winner of an example for prosperity.

> Am I attracting prosperity into my life? Yes!
> When? Now!
> How? Through self-love and self-discipline!

Another example, on a slightly lighter side.
> Am I losing weight? Yes!
> When? Now!
> How? Through self-love and self-discipline!

Here's how it works. You ask yourself three questions. The first one practices self forgiveness and immediately puts a positive outcome in place of the negative behavior or situation. It sets your mind in a better direction. Saying YES, is your internal commitment to a winning result.

The second question 'When?' deals with making it happen in the present moment. It is the most critical step taking away thoughts of delaying – procrastination.

'How?' is the cherry on top of the cake. This third questions raises you above the idea that the outside world controls you and places the power of your thoughts and actions right back where they belong – inside you!

You've now set the direction, fueled your desires with self-empowerment in this moment. Isn't Making love With Life discovering ways to live and love yourself in the moment! Yes!

> TIP: The beauty of this is that you don't need anything more than a small card to put it on and carry it with you, wherever you go. Post notes throughout your home and office, with Flexible Affirmations and read them daily. I post them in the bathroom, kitchen, car, office, anywhere I use a space frequently.

Expressions of the love offering kind

Diamonds are a girls best friend!?
What if it is the size of a baseball?
Richard Burton spent $1,050,000 to buy a 69.42 Carat diamond from Cartier, for Elizabeth Taylor. Other baubles he bought for Elizabeth include the 33.9 carat Krupp diamond ($350,000), the Ping-Pong diamond ($38,000), La Peregrina pearl ($37,000), an emerald ($93,000), a $65,000 sapphire brooch and at $125,000 the most expensive mink coat in the world. Those prices were when a buck was worth a buck. Now that's what I call a big spender! They got married in Montreal, Quebec, Canada.

Ponder this

Is political correctness one of the greatest evils inflicted upon humanity? Is it a form of denial and conformity, attempting to create pasteurized human thought? Is it like genetic inbreeding? Does it carry a price far beyond it's mandate? Is this when the wolf discovers how to disguise itself as a sheep? Does one no longer hear the authentic voice of another?

If yes is your answer to any one of these questions then watch out. You may step on one or more landmines of the hidden agenda. You may get blown away before you even realize what happened.

Free yourself – be authentic.

Improve your life with a
Live Loving and Love Living journaling experience

Become your own best friend. Discover a mental breath of fresh air. Use journaling to create better self-awareness.

How? You write letters to yourself about your feelings, thoughts, activities and ideas.

The benefits of this process include: greater self-awareness, organization of thoughts, problem solving and setting attainable goals. In addition, your writing and communication skills improve.

Getting started is easy. Get a spiral note pad or fancy bound book with blank pages. Next, sit down and write. Spelling and grammar are not important. Let your creative juices flow. Don't censor yourself. This is your gift to yourself.

A great opening is today's date. Then write… Dear Self. I end all my letters with… Love, Ken. For the best results write anytime, anywhere and often. This is a portable activity. A private and quiet place is recommended, but not necessary. Express your feelings – happy, worry, content, scared, excited, sad, confused, etc. – in writing. You may need practice in getting in tune with your inner self.

Many start by writing their activities and expanding upon them. Thoughts, ideas and feelings start flowing freely after awhile. Questions and problems appear clearer once committed to paper. Like magic, solutions start revealing themselves to you. Ninety percent of the answer to most questions lies in the questions. This process lets you constantly reframe your thinking and perceptions.

Eventually you enter a state of conscious continuous self-improvement and focus – a form of directed consciousness. Giving yourself permission to remove the distractions and noise of daily life, adds clarity to your life. Start your journal today, you'll be happy you did.

TIP.   Make a contract with yourself to do it for at least 21 days.

SPECIAL OFFER: Get a journal you can carry with you all the time. *The Make Love With Life Journal,* AGES Publications, contains a quick tip ten point journal course, over 100 inspirational sayings and blank pages. Fits neatly in purses, briefcases, almost anything. Your investment is only $7.95. Tell them where you read this to get free shipping and handling! To order *The Make Love With Life Journal,* call toll free 1-800-263-1991.

An 'Ah-Ha!' story

DANCING WITH I.V.

The intravenous tube snaked its way into my vein.

'I had been violated!' my voice screamed in my head.

Vaguely, I remember Stephanie, my eight year old, turning and asking her mom, "Is Daddy dying?" Such is the power of dehydration, pneumonia and hallucinations combined. It's one big pain.

I had been in the emergency area of the hospital for six hours. At last, the tests confirmed it. I was sick. Only then was my lifeline to recovery, the intravenous needle, inserted. Its tall slender stainless steel body snaked skyward from my prone position in the hospital bed. In its arms were a saline solution and antibiotic pump, dripping their life force of fluids into my bloodstream... nurturing my body's strength, as one lover does for another.

Feebly, I pushed myself out of the bed. I grasped the intravenous pole's cool curvaceous figure in my right hand, and stumbled toward the bathroom. Fortunately IV's feet remained steadfastly grounded as we glided onward.

My 5 and 8 year old pride and joys, Alan and Stephanie, watched with a mixture of fear then joy as I went from novice to professional and mastered waltzing with my IV. At least she let me lead once I was ready.

> The pain of the past can become an illusion

Such are the adversities of life we all overcome. Showing the children that our attitude matters... that we can stand on our own two feet when adversity strikes... That is how they best learn.

Oh yeah, about my partner IV, we created quite a stir, a magical mood arose as we danced the dance of life, winding our way down the hospitals halls, led by the children's song, "Daddy is dancing with IV, Daddy is..."

 **P**onder this

> A mind that is stretched to a new idea,
> never returns to its original dimensions.
>
> Oliver Wendell Holmes

Life, how sweet it is!?

Try this grass and you'll be amazed! That's right – sweet grass, *stevia,* is an ancient natural grass sugar concentrate. So sweet that a pinch is all you need. It's low in calories and has none of the known side effects of white processed sugar or artificial sweeteners like aspartame.

The sweetness is slightly different and it takes a bit to get used to it, but that is a small price to pay for something that gives you the benefits of sweetness with almost none of the calories or side effects of what we commonly use daily.

I started using it slowly in herbal teas, in unsweetened Kool Aid, then various other things. Breaking free from the traditional sweeteners takes time.

This is how plant life makes love with humans in subtle yet powerful ways. This partnership is an evolutionary process which enhances life rather than takes from it.

A world wide soft drink manufacturer used *stevia* in their calorie reduced pop in Japan for many years. A corporate decision was made by them to standardize their product around the world. Out went *stevia*. In went artificial sweeteners.

In the movie *The Lion King* by Disney Studios, they mentioned sweet grass. The indigenous Guarani Indians of Paraguay call *stevia* the *Honey Leaf.* They grow and use it for dietary and healing purposes. Natural Ways Products of Utah produces stevia products found in health food stores.

A small amount can last a very long time, considering that it is hundreds of times sweeter by volume than cane and beet sugars or artificial sweeteners . Where do you get *stevia?* Try your local health food store.

P.S. I'll place an order for the first mass market cook book that shows how to use *stevia* as the main sweetener in cooking, baking and other foods. It's stability and safety offers numerous advantages over the artificial sweeteners food processors and suppliers use, without any of their side effects. If you know of a good cook book using *stevia*, please write me c/o of the publisher at the address at the end of the book, so I can share the good news with all the readers of future Make Love With Life books in the Love Living and Live Loving Series.

How sweet it is – let's *stevia* it and see!

One persons perception of perfection is anothers poison.

First aid... For the Hugging Deficient

Years ago, my Mom become one of the first official huggers for premature babies at the local hospital. She had gone through quite a rigorous application and interview process before being chosen for this volunteer position. Training was mandatory.

Her reward – an hour in the nursery to hug a child to health and wellbeing. Research indicated that the survival rate for premature babies and their rate of growth increased significantly when they were frequently and lovingly held and cuddled. Incidentally, studies by a group specializing in geriatric care in a Florida golden age home found that those who gave got as good a benefit, if not a greater benefit, as those who received.

Hugging deficient!? Embrace this idea today. Become a volunteer hugger at a hospital, geriatric home or other places where the hugging deficient are hiding out.

> PS.   Mom's since graduated to helping and hugging cancer patients at the hospital.

To wait for someone else, or to expect someone else to make life richer, or fuller, or more satisfying, puts me in a constant state of suspension – and I miss all those moments that pass.

They never come back to be experienced again.

Kathleen Crilly

Why is it...

When I was a kid,
people looked lots older
Now that I am older,
older people look rather younger to me.

Enrich your life

Before you go to bed tonight, list five things you are grateful for. They can be the simplest of things – a roof over your head, a warm bed to sleep in, clean water, food, a smile you put on someone's face, the simple fact that you are alive. Reconnect to the wonder of being alive, each and every night. Take nothing for granted.

P.S.   Say a little prayer for this to become a kinder and gentler world. Every thought counts.

Tip: Get *The Make Love With Life Journal* to record your life affirming activities and experience. You'll discover it is an inviting journal with a difference.

Become a silver haired gigolo!

First cruise lines did it. Then ballrooms did it. Now senior centers and retirement homes are hiring foxy silver haired men to dance with the ladies, to liven up the parties. The large lack of older men who can dance, helped create a booming industry in 'Retiree hoofers-for-hire.' Now you can vacation in sunny Florida and earn a few bucks on the side. Is that what they mean by play as they pay?

Quick pick me up

Treat yourself to a facial, manicure or pedicure today. A good idea is to treat a friend to one today. Better idea is to share the experience by both of you getting facials, manicures and pedicures at the same time.

Hot tip: Best idea. Saves money also. Creates a bond of friendship. Do a facial, manicure or pedicure for each other. Then switch roles. Go for it – do all three at once for each other. …It's great fun!

Do a living video journal

One day I asked my father-in-law if he'd mind me recording an interview of him by his daughter and the children. He is generally a private person, but relented and said yes.

At first the questions and answers came slowly, then he started enjoying sharing his wisdom. Here are some of the questions asked. They can get you started.

What are the five best books you ever read?

Share five happy things that you remember?

What were your favorite foods, when you were a kid?

What were the greatest inventions or discoveries during your life time?

Tell me about the most awesome new events that happened during your life?

What's the funniest thing you remember? best joke? best sunset? best_____?

What was the silliest thing you did as a kid? adult?

By now I hope you get the idea. Have fun and get your loved ones on video now. Plan to do it once a year with friends, your kids, family, any one you want to remember fondly. Do it while they are still alive and healthy.

Trivia of the least important kind

A poll reported in *Redbook* asked couples:

Would you lend out your spouse for a night for a million dollars?

"No way," said two out of three.
"I'd consider it and give it some thought," replied 16%.
"It's a deal," said one out of ten.

Three affirmations for a better today

I see only the good points in others.

I am not attached to the past and live in the now!

There is infinite power within me to have a great day.

Liberating thing you can do

Give up the need to be right. …How?

Use these three attitude fixers in whatever situations of conflict that arise.

Reconciliation, Reconciliation and Reconciliation.

I believe in the sun even when it is not shining

I believe in love even when feeling it not.

I believe in God even when he is silent.

Hebrew Prayer

Invite yourself to a friends house to make them supper. I like to do Italian or Chinese Wok cooking and salads. Bring along the fixings and have them set the table. Set the mood with candles, a potted plant, flowers or a balloon for a center piece. Create the mood.

Health tip trivia of the most important kind.

The Harvard Health letter of February 1996 indicated that researchers found a strong correlation between loss of vision and consumption of saturated fats.

TIP: Bilberry, an herb was used with WW II fighter pilots to help their vision. Particularly beneficial for farsighted folks and improving night vision.

Thought to ponder today

To give voice to the voiceless... To give life to the lifeless... To give hope to the hopeless... is our quest – our reason for being – so all may be healed.

It is then, and only then that humanity will have risen above itself. No longer reaching for the stars, but at last being a shining example and star in its own right. Heaven on earth.

Food trivia of the most interesting kind
When is a tomato not a vegetable?

Always. Tomatoes, are technically berries – fruits. A long time ago, when they didn't have personal income tax, food taxes or tariffs were a main source of revenue. Tomatoes got categorized as vegetables for tax revenue purposes.

"To label me is to hide what I am behind a garment of confusion."

Trivia of the most important kind
The Healing Power of Love

Anorexia nervosa is a life threatening condition. The ABC network on the show 20/20 featured the Mantreaux Clinic in Victoria, British Columbia, Canada. Why? Primarily using the power of love and validation, they have been able to save loads of victims of this possibly fatal condition. Hospitals failed miserably in terms of their success rates when compared to this clinic's rate of success.

Proof once again that love is the answer.

Discover the trick for seeing what makes another person tick when it comes to love?

Easy. Watch how they express their love then mirror them. If they touch to express themselves, then touch back. If they use words, then use words. This is a super secret for building relationships. In essence, to see how to love another, watch how they express love – then do it.

Absolute attention is prayer.

Zen saying

Quick stress reducing techniques, that can help get you revved up for lovemaking with life or a partner.

Stress causes blood to flow toward the limbs from the central body and sexual organs. This can result in a reduced sex drive as well as lose of pleasure in making love with life. To reduce the affects of stress, try these quick methods.

Drink water. Stress causes sweating which leads to feeling dehydrated. At bedtime, drink at least two glasses of water and you'll feel better.

Straighten yourself out. Many people slouch when they are stressed which reduces blood flow and restricts breathing. Sitting up straight helps you breath easier and get more life enhancing oxygen into your brain.

Deep breathing. Press your palms against your legs or each other. Keep a steady pressure on your hands and take a deep breath through your nose and hold it in for five seconds. Slowly exhale through your lips and at the same time let your hands relax. Repeat this five to ten times, stopping once you feel relaxed.

TIP: Great before lovemaking or anytime you need to boost your life force energy.

Energize your body with Asparagus!?

Rich in potassium, calcium and phosphorus which are needed for maintenance of a high energy level. It contains a diuretic that increases the amount of excreted urine and excites the urinary passages. However, another component of asparagus, aspartic acid, neutralizes excess amounts of ammonia in the body. Ammonia may cause sexual disinterest and apathy.

Secret for life long happiness

When you do something for someone else, do it out of love – expect nothing in return.

Trivia of the most important kind

Discover the deliciously addictive nature of oxytocin! It's legal! It's yours for the sharing.

Create your own natural high with the healing power of touch. It can boost your immune system. Tame your blood pressure. Plus a whole bunch of other life and love affirming emotional and physical benefits!

In the book, *The Alchemy of Love and Lust* (Putnam), Dr. Theresa Crenshaw, a San Diego, California, physician and sex therapist, says oxytocin is a natural chemical secreted by the pituitary gland when our skin is touched. It flows through male and female brains and reproductive tracts. The more you are touched, the more your body craves it – thus enhancing bonding.

It is safe, healthy and healing. Interestingly women's bodies release a larger dose than do men's bodies. Maybe this explains why women want cuddling more and men want sex.

So shall the 'twain meet – share a hug today!

Do this quick prosperity check up
   you'll be amazed at the results.

Tools: Pen and paper.
In one column, put all the years you have worked.
Beside each year, put what you earned.
Total all the earnings.

Surprised at how much money has passed through your hands? If you earn an average of $25,000 a year and work 40 years, that's a million dollars!

The point is enjoy your life now – you're already rich!

Health Myth trivia of the most important kind

 Dr. Bhiku Jethalal said one only has to look at elephants and cows, which are vegetarians, to know that it is a myth that a meatless diet cannot provide enough protein.

TIP: Combine beans and rice, or eat lentils or soybean based products to get the protein you need. After a short while your system will adjust to eating and digesting beans and gas will become a thing of the past - no pun intended.

Vegetarians, should check their B12 levels and occasionally supplement with a B12 vitamin, according to health practitioners.

Nuts are also a wonderful source of protein, as well as peas, cereals, wheat, nut preparations and cow peas.

Enrich your life

Here's a simple goal setting technique to enrich your life and get you on the move, so to speak

S.C.R.A.M. — goals that are
Specific, Concrete, Realistic, Attainable and Measurable.

Got a dream, make the first step and set it in motion.

Life, believe, is not a dream
 So dark as sages say;
  Oft a little morning rain
   Foretells a pleasant day.

Charlotte Bronte

The cheap psychiatrist
 Breaking free of the past.

Our lives are filled with repeated conditioned responses. The key is to become aware of them, in particular those from our childhoods. A great technique for dealing with fears is to confront them. Here's an example.

If you consistently experienced humiliation in your childhood, it may be the reason you have trouble speaking in public or communicating intimately with others. Finding the voice who made you feel little, is a step in the right direction. This is not about blame, but about airing your buried feelings and confronting the repeated experiences that made you how you are today.

The next step is what is called the chair exercise. Get an empty chair. Sit or stand facing the chair. Close your eyes and see the person who made you feel this way. You are now going to share with them, how they made you feel. If it is anger, humiliation, fear anything that has stopped you from being who you want to be – then talk with them. Let them know how you felt and how you feel. Do this repeatedly until you feel you've vented enough.

Now, focus on the outcome you would like to see. Tell them what you are going to become. Share your plans, hopes and desires. Think of it as a dialogue, where you are moving from where you are now to where you want to be.

A step in the right direction, since you are now consciously mastering your destiny.

Keys to diffuse tension

Active listening skills are one of the best ways to diffuse tension and the accompanying stress. Here are keys to putting them into practice

Stop what your doing – all activities. Make your posture physically inviting, open to receiving. Make direct eye contact.

Show your interested using facial expressions. Encourage the speaker nonverbally as well as verbally.

Identify the content of the persons message. Identify their feelings and unstated messages.

Clarify what you heard. Paraphrase what was said. Verify what you heard.

Ponder this

We are not human beings learning to be spiritual;
we are spiritual beings learning to be human.

Pierre Teilhard de Chardin

Try this birthday celebrations with a twist

Getting older beats the alternative. Aging is something to be celebrated.

Here's a unique approach. Rather than getting gifts, give them instead. Being thankful is one of the simplest ways for acknowledging all life has to offer. Next time it is your birthday, anniversary or any celebration invite everyone and give them small gifts or tokens of your appreciation.

> TIP: To make this even more valuable, ask them to do the same thing for their birthdays.

The difference between gifts of obligation and those of love, is quite large.

Discover... the Law of Detachment

Powerful... Simple... Effective... This idea helps you deal with any negative vibrations affecting your sense of serenity and peaceful coexistence with the universe.

These are the four D's to apply when dealing with life problems such as divorce, criticism or someone else's anger.

Detach yourself from events.

Decide to focus on love or positive outcomes.

Divide assets – treat inanimate things as just that, treat them as objects.

Deal with your own stuff.

This is how Joyce, an attendee at my seminar at the Celebration Center of Religious Science in Fall Church, Virginia, summarized the idea called Divorce, the Healing Relationship, that I shared with them.

Life is like a can of worms. To many this has a negative connotations. In reality it has a positive outcome
— rich fertile earth.

Follow that hunch

"Intuition is the immediate knowing of something without the use of conscious reasoning," according to Webster's New World Dictionary.

Use this problem solving technique. Start tapping into intuition today. Try this five step approach.

1. Experience and knowledge are the foundation of intuition. Do your homework.
2. Submerge yourself in the question, then back off.
3. Relax and detach yourself from the question.

4. What you know best is what gives you the best hunches. Trust your experience. Accept the hunch as a new approach to your question. Don't let your inner censor discard it before further examining it.

5. Check your hunch out a second time, before acting upon it. Think of it as a new opening strategy giving you a fresh insight into the question, situation or problem.

The great secret known to doctors, but still hidden from the general public, is that if you let it be, your body has a wisdom to naturally heal itself - and in most cases will. This is what making love with life is all about.

It is based on the ancient knowledge of Hippocrates. "Heal thyself," he wrote. Ask any honest internist and that's what they'll tell you.

The movement toward alternative self-health care is the key behind medical practitioners such as Julian Whittaker, R. Willix, Atkins, Deepak Chopra, Andrew Weil, Bernie Siegel and numerous other doctors who discovered ancient knowledge and truths that are being born out by modern research. They are very effective solutions for many health problems.

Trivia of the most important kind
or why folks are turning to vegetarianism

The amount of water consumed by and used to produce food for a meat eating American is 608,000 gallons each year. This is 10 times more water than is consumed to produce the beans, grains and vegetables for vegetarians.

Maybe instead of water rationing, they should have meatless months?

Your living is determined not so much by what life brings you as by the attitude you bring to life; not so much by what happens to you as by the way your mind looks at what happens.

John Miller

We are just tenants on this planet, waiting for the new landlords to take over — our children.

An 'Ah-Ha!' story with a poetic bent

THEY CAME...

They came for the Communists,
  and I didn't object —
    For I was not a Communist;

They came for the Socialists,
  and I didn't object —
    For I was not a Socialist;

They came for the labor leaders,
  and I didn't object —
    For I was not a labor leader;

The came for the Jews,
  and I didn't object —
    For I was not a Jew;

They came for me —
  And there was no one left to object.

> Silence,
> like denial,
> is a
> three sided sword.
>
> The price
> you pay tomorrow
> may exceed the cost
> of your silence
> today.

Comment made during the second world war, by the German Protestant pastor, Martin Neimoller.

Trivia of the most important kind

The value of all oil, coal and gas consumed in the USA is less than the value of raw materials used to produce food from livestock, according to a 1978 study sponsored by the U.S. department of Interior and Commerce.

TIP: If everyone had one more meatless meal a week, this would have an incredibly positive affect, on our environment. Want to know more, check out John Robbins books, *Diet for a New America* and *Diet for a New World*.

We trek to every conceivable corner of consciousness and the planet in search of wholeness.

All along the answers lie deep within our own bodies.

Dr. Christiane Northrup

Do...Do More

Do more than exist – live.
Do more than touch – feel.
Do more than look – observe.
Do more than read – absorb.
Do more than hear – listen
Do more than listen – understand.
Do more than think – ponder.
Do more than talk – say something.

John Rhoades

Seek wholeness in relationships.

Start out from a position of being and accepting whom you are. Move away from the possession model, which is a form of consumerism. Move toward that which is a way of celebrating each others uniqueness.

Setting the tone

Music is an incredible tool to help you live in the moment. Here are some unique labels, artists and titles I've discovered for you.

On the Hearts of Space, San Francisco, CA label:
Black Marbel & Sweet Fire by Al Khan & Kai Taschner
Yearning by Robert Rich & Lisa Moskow
Angels of the Deep by Raphael

On the SOCAN Montreal, Canada label:
Cristal Silence by Robert Coxon

These musicians works help you discover a higher state of consciousness and revitalized perception. Ask for them in your local music store, if you're looking for something different and inviting.

Trivia of the most important kind

Women, 65 years of age and older, who eat vegetarian diets were found to have half the bone loss compared to women eating a regular meat based diet. They were less likely to break bones, they healed quicker, had better posture and were more active.

Which came first the vegetarian or the healthier body? I'm too chicken to take a guess.

Health trivia of the most important kind

The amount of water used by a 1,000 pound steer that is brought to market, is enough to float a destroyer, according to Newsweek Magazine.

Celebrate Earth Day

Join the largest environmental party on the face of the Earth. Worldwide, April 22 is officially known as Earth Day.

The ability to consciously practice thankfulness is one of humanities greatest gifts. Acknowledging our oneness with the universe is humbling.

Idea: Make a donation to an environmental group. Get a group together to clean up areas that humans have fowled. At the very least take a moment of silence to honor Mother Earth, as she honors us - her tenants.

P.S. Make every day a celebration of Earth Day

Ponder this

Knowledge is gained by learning;
trust by doubt; and love by love.

Thomas Szasz

Trivia of the questioning kind

"A third of the world's fish catch, 80 % of the worlds corn and 95% of the worlds oats are fed to livestock," writes Atlas Seager, in his book *State of the Environment,* Penguin Books.

Thought provoking questions:
Does this suggest a solution to the problem of hunger in the world?

Could all be fed?

Idea: What if we all wrote or called MacDonald's, Burger King, Harvey's and Wendy's and asked them to include more vegetarian choices on their menus? Think of all the children who would not have to starve, so that we may be fed.

Thought for today

Pharmacological medicine is based on a system of patent protection and manipulation of natural healing chemicals. Traditional medicine is less than a century old. In fact, it is a misnomer to call it traditional. Alternative medicine is better known as complementary medicine because all healing should work together to create a better life for people.

Economic forces and the fact that medicine shifted from primarily being a healing profession to a business, created an unbalanced set of methods and treatments. Doctors, who do not follow the pharmacological model of big business, run the risk of losing their license to practice their livelihood. This threat is enough to keep most in line.

Over 75% of drug companies revenues are generated in the USA and Canada. In the rest of the world, numerous other methods are used. Western medicine is used to complement other healing systems.

An 'Ah-Ha!' story

YOUR CUP RUNNETH OVER

A renowned professor of philosophy was granted a meeting with the Dalai Lama, a great spiritual leader. He was ushered into the simple office, with little pomp and ceremony, this being an informal meeting.

Excitedly the professor began to question and bombard the holy man with information. Finally, the Dalai Lama raised his hand to silence the visitor. "Would you like some tea?" he asked.

"Yes," replied the professor, as he continued to babble. The Dalai Lama filled his cup, then proceeded to fill

> The symphony of life is best heard in the silences between the notes.

the Professor's cup. He did not stop as the tea began spilling over the teacup's sides, making a lake upon the table top.

"Your spilling the tea!" exclaimed the professor.

The Dalai Lama stopped and said, "So is the mind that is so full of chatter that it cannot quiet itself nor hear humanity's songs of delight. To the quieted mind, all things are known."

To dishonor another is to dishonor yourself. To honor another, is to honor yourself. Honor yourself and honor the universe. Payment in kind will be your reward.

Point to ponder

Presentology, what I call my idea of living in the moment, is a most powerful way of savoring life. Being present is manifested in meditation for many. Meditation is a heightened state of directed consciousness. First, one must direct themselves inward so that they may finally and fully connect themselves with the universe. Presentology is no more than the study of what it takes to arrive at that state of being. In a Kabalistic or a mystical sense this means being egoless, so that one may be fully present – free of the need to be right and to need to know... liberated.

In *The Ultimate Power: How to Unlock Your Mind-Body-Soul Potential* (AGES Publications) I created a self-help therapeutic path, based on my life experience in overcoming a few adversities. I term it Neiatherapy, which loosely translated means Now Therapy. Fortunately individuals and groups are using and expanding this model. Learning how to live in the moment is one of the incredibly powerful and fulfilling ideas it releases.

Poem to ponder, today and for the rest of your life. Changed to honor women.

IF...

If you can keep your head when all about you
Are losing theirs and blaming it on you,
If you can trust yourself when all women doubt you
But make allowances for their doubting too;
If you can wait and not be tired by waiting,
Or being lied about, don't deal in lies,
Or being hated, don't give way to hating,
And yet don't look too good, nor talk too wise:
If you can dream – and not make dreams your master:
If you can think – and not make thoughts your aim:
If you can meet with triumph and disaster
And treat those two impostors just the same.
If you can make one heap of all your winnings
And risk it on one turn of pitch and toss,
And lose, and start again at your beginnings
And never breath a word about your loss.
If you can talk with crowds and keep your virtue,
Or walk with Queens – nor lose the common touch,
If neither foes nor loving friends can hurt you.
If all women count with you, but none too much;
If you can fill the unforgiving minute
With sixty seconds' worth of distance run,
Yours is the Earth and everything that's in it,
And – which is more – you'll be a Woman, whose won!

My apologies to Rudyard Kipling,
the British writer and poet, who created this poem.
To honor my daughter, mother and all those women in my life,
I changed the poem's gender.

107

<u>To Write To The Author</u>

Dear Reader, Meeting Planner, or Speakers' Bureau

Both the author and publisher appreciate hearing from you and learning of the benefits and enjoyment you received from this book. We cannot guarantee that every letter written can be answered by the author, but all will be forwarded. To help ensure that your letter is answered, or to arrange a speaking engagement or seminar, please write to the appropriate address below.

Make your convention or meeting a memorable experience. Book Ken Vegotsky as your Keynote Speaker or seminar/workshop facilitator. He is an entertaining educator. A good time is guaranteed for all!

Ken says, "May I always give you more than you pay for. May you always want to pay me more."

That is Ken's philosophy and a fact!

In the U.S.A.

Ken Vegotsky
c/o AGES Publications™
8391 Beverly Blvd., #323-ML
Los Angeles, CA 90048
Please enclose a self-addressed, stamped envelop for reply,
and $3.00 to cover costs.

In Canada

Ken Vegotsky
c/o AGES Publications™
1054-2 Centre St., #153-ML
Thornhill, Ontario, Canada L4J 8E5.
Please enclose a self-addressed, stamped envelop for reply,
and $4.00 to cover costs.

If outside the U.S.A. or Canada

Enclose international postal reply coupon with a
self-addressed envelope and $3.00 U.S. to cover costs.

Contact Coordinator – phone (519) 396-9553 – fax (519) 396-9554

A Great Gift for the
Special People In Your Life!

The Ultimate Power

A National Bestseller!
ISBN 1-886508-15-1

The Way You Look at Life
— and Death —
Will Never Be The Same

Take Control of Your Life
Become the Master of Your Destiny
Learn the Secrets of Living on Your Own Terms
Utilize Your Mind-Body-Soul Potential to
Gain Complete Happiness

"Wow – what a great book. If you are ready to turn on your Ultimate Power, read Ken's brilliant and illuminating book."

Mark Victor Hansen
co-author of Chicken Soup for the Soul
New York Times #1 Bestseller

"As a psychologist – and a human being – I recommend The Ultimate Power to people who suffer chronic pain as well as to people who are searching for their authentic voice and a new beginning to life."

Dr. J. Siegel, Psychologist

"Ken Vegotsky has written a GREAT book. A heroic book. He is the Victor Frankl of our day. You will want to purchase many copies to give to those you love, those who are discouraged, those who need to rise again from adversity."

Dottie Walters, President
Walters International Speakers Bureau
Author of Speak & Grow Rich

From AGES Publications

**Books
+
Audio Tapes**

The Ultimate Power

An eight cassette audio tape program. Includes the book. For you, a friend or a study group.

Hypnotic Journey of Gentle Surrender

A combination of guided imagery, breathing techniques and music. Relaxation techniques that can improve your emotional and physical sense of well being. Aid to better sleeping and living life more fully in the moment.

The Gift of Laughter

The laughter of children mingled with the music of a babbling brook. Just plain old fun, helping to rekindle the child within.

Order Form

BOOKS	Qty	Price	Total
The Make Love With Life Journal over 100 inspirational & motivational sayings		$7.95	
222 Ways to Make Love With Life How To Love, Laugh and Live in the Moment		$7.95	
222 More Ways to Make Love With Life More Ways for Loving... Living in the Moment		$7.95	
For Lovers Only 222 Ways to Enhance the Magic		$7.95	
222 Ways to Stress Free Living Reduce Stress and Make Love With Life		$7.95	
The Ultimate Power How to Unlock Your Mind Body Soul Potential		$14.95	
AUDIO TAPES			
The Ultimate Power – 8 cassettes program includes the book		$89.95	
Hypnotic Journey of Gentle Surrender – Relaxation techniques		$9.95	
The Gift of Laughter helping to rekindle the child within		$9.95	
Special Offer – all audio tapes Save over $10 now!		$99.00	
Sub-total			
(over $36 free delivery or $3.00 for 1st item + $0.50 for each additional item) Shipping			
Total			

Name_____

Address _____

City _____ZIP _____

Phone _____

Please make certified check/money order payable to and send to
Adi, Gaia, Esalen Publications Inc.
8391 Beverly St. #323-ML, Los Angeles, CA 90048

VISA ❏   MasterCard ❏   American Express ❏

Call Toll free 1-800-263-1991
Overseas call (519) 396-9553 or Fax (519) 396-9554

About the Author...

Ken Vegotsky

...is a professional speaker, author and entrepreneur. Ken has given keynote addresses and seminars in the U.S.A. and Canada. He has been featured in print, radio and TV in the U.S.A., Canada, Australia, New Zealand, United Kingdom and a host of other countries.

"Ken is the Victor Frankl of our day," noted Dottie Walters, President of Walters Speakers Bureau and author of *Speak & Grow Rich.*

Mark Victor Hansen, New York Times #1 bestselling co-author of the *Chicken Soup for the Soul,* says Ken's work is, *"Brilliant and Illuminating."*

"In recognition of being seen as a model of courage and hope for others, who demonstrates to all of us the nobility of the human spirit..." begins the Clarke Institute Psychiatric Foundation nomination of Ken for a *Courage To Come Back Award.* These awards were originated by the St. Francis Health Foundation of Pittsburgh, PA.

Ken has served on the boards of NACPAC (affiliate of the American Chronic Pain Association) and a half-way home for mentally challenged people in transition. After numerous inspirational speeches, Ken was encouraged by listeners to tell his story.

His National Bestseller, *The Ultimate Power* shares his captivating first-person account of his near-death experience, garnished with proven keys for unlocking your personal power.

Dicover *How to Make Love With Life*™ and you'll feel embraced by caring and compassion as you share his moving experience.

To arrange a keynote, seminar and/or workshop presentation by Ken Vegotsky call the contact coordinator at (519) 396-9553.